Reinventing Communication

Mark Phillips' method on the use of communications theory to improve program planning and execution has the potential of being a game changer for successful program management teams. All program and technical managers should read and apply the ideas in Reinventing Communication.

Gordon Kranz, US Office of the Secretary of Defense

It is an unfortunate trait of the program management community that often more time is spent analyzing what went wrong than what went right and why ... Mr Phillips turns that tide with a book that is actionable—earned value and a communications strategy are key. In Reinventing Communication, *the author analyzes successful programs and failed programs. He answers the question—what are the attributes of success? Further, he offers a checklist and an actionable approach to delivering a success in which communications and earned value management are effective tools.*

Vice Admiral Joseph W. Dyer, USN (ret.),
former Commander, Naval Air Systems Command

Mark Phillips practically invented project management for web companies. In his new book, Mark shares his latest research on creating the right environment for attaining ambitious results. He draws on economics, psychology, project management and decades of experience as a CEO and thought leader. The stories alone make the book worth reading. It is a must-have for web companies, entrepreneurs and established companies who want to maintain an edge.

Ilya Pozin, columnist, *Forbes & Inc.*

Just as we were about to conclude that computers and technology have preempted the future contribution of homo sapiens, here comes a book that explains how effective communication and human interaction will always win the day. If you are embarking on a project, any project, you must read Reinventing Communication *first.*

Ed Brodow, author of *Negotiation Boot Camp*

A must-read book, Mark's commonsense methodologies and knowledgeable approaches to project management, leadership, and increased communication skills makes this a great guide for any entrepreneur, business owner, engineer, or developer who wants to be a more successful leader within any business, project, or market area.

Bruce Holmes, US Navy SEAL (ret.),
Science and Technology Advisor

Powerful and practical, Mark Phillips' new book, Reinventing Communication, *breaks our common misconceptions about project performance and carves a bold, new path in management. The book shows you how to create, lead and manage successful projects. It is a rare find, brimming with strategies and ideas you can use immediately to deliver better results.*

Cornelius Fichtner, The PM Podcast

Reinventing Communication

How to Design, Lead and Manage High Performing Projects

MARK PHILLIPS

Routledge
Taylor & Francis Group

LONDON AND NEW YORK

First published 2014 by Gower Publishing

2 Park Square, Milton Park, Abingdon, Oxon OX14 4RN
711 Third Avenue, New York, NY 10017, USA

Routledge is an imprint of the Taylor & Francis Group, an informa business

First issued in paperback 2016

British Library Cataloguing in Publication Data
A catalogue record for this book is available from the British Library.

Library of Congress Cataloging-in-Publication Data
Phillips, Mark (Mark Andrew)
  Reinventing communication : how to design, lead and manage high performing projects /
by Mark Phillips.
    pages cm
  Includes bibliographical references and index.
  ISBN 978-1-4724-1100-6 (hardback)
  1. Project management. 2. Communication in management. I. Title.
  HD69.P75P495 2014
  658.4'04–dc23

                                                                          2013045591

ISBN 978-1-4724-1100-6 (hbk)
ISBN 978-1-138-27007-7 (pbk)

Contents

List of Figures   *vii*

List of Tables   *ix*

About the Author   *xi*

Preface and Acknowledgments   *xiii*

Glossary   *xvii*

Introduction   Communication as a Project Performance
Management Tool   1

PART I   WHY COMMUNICATION MATTERS

1   Communication Determines Project Outcomes   13

2   Elements of Communication Design   21

3   Communication Objects and Communication Design   39

4   Observable Behaviors of a Project Environment   57

5   Using Communication as a Performance
Management Tool   69

6   A Checklist for Using Communication as a
Performance Management Tool   85

PART II   COMMUNICATION MANAGES PROJECT COMPLEXITY

7   Orientation Toward Uncertainty   107

8   All Uncertainty is Wicked   129

Appendix   Case Study: An IT Department Supporting a
Large Project   139

Index   *153*

List of Figures

| 2.1 | Increasing Definition Improves Outcomes | 30 |

3.1	Retweet Activity by Hour	42
3.2	Day of the Week Impact on E-mail Click-throughs	43
3.3	Click-through Rate by Links Tweeted per Hour	45

5.1	Communication Integrated with a PMB	72
5.2	P COM and A COM for Scenario Two	77
5.3	P COM and A COM for Scenario Three	77

| 6.1 | CTRs by Hour | 94 |

A.1	A Comparison of Known Issues with Numbers of E-mails	148
A.2	Open Rates for E-mails over Time	150
A.3	Reply Rates to E-mails over Time	151

List of Figures

List of Tables

5.1   Estimate of the Number of E-mails Generated over a
            Given Period   71
5.2   Cumulative Values of P COM and A COM for Scenarios One,
            Two and Three   74
5.3   COM V for Each of the Three Scenarios at Specific Points
            in Time   75

6.1   Using Communication as a Performance Management Tool   86
6.2   A Sample Cataloging of the Analytical and Management
            Parameters for Several Communication Methods   99

7.1   Observable Manifestations of Orientation Toward Uncertainty   125

About the Author

Mark Phillips is an accomplished CEO and thought leader. For over 17 years he has built a project management software company and consultancy, serving clients including multinational automotives, web start-ups, global telecoms and financial services. He led product development on a cutting-edge US Army Research Lab program.

Mark is known for finding and delivering innovative solutions. His ideas are in use at the Office of the Secretary of Defense to research new policy guidelines on performance management and improve program outcomes. His work has appeared in publications including C|Net, eWeek and the *Small Wars Journal*. He delivers keynotes, seminars and workshops worldwide. He is a board member of the College of Performance Management. Mark began his career on Wall Street where he was a Vice President.

Mark holds a Masters in Applied Economics from the University of Michigan and a BSc [Econ] from the London School of Economics. Visit Mark at www.communicationmeasurement.org.

Preface and Acknowledgments

This book proposes a method to analyze, design, manage and lead Project Environments. It is based on the centrality of communication in determining project outcomes and the inherently social aspect of all Project Environments. The concepts it covers are useful for managers, project managers, systems engineers and leaders. People who work in Project Environments will also find it useful in helping them understand and navigate the environment in which they operate.

We start out by describing the role of communication in determining project outcomes. From there we move on to describing observable elements we can track and measure that reflect the Communication Environment. Next we describe the observable elements of Communication Objects. These are observable behaviors of people who receive the communication. These tell us what people do with the communication they receive. We then spend time describing a fundamental design element, orientation toward uncertainty, which impacts a Project Environment's behavior and choices. This leads us to an understanding of the primacy social elements play in determining project outcomes.

A Note about Jargon

Throughout the book we will refer to Project Environments instead of single projects. The term "Project Environment" recognizes the wide range of factors that influence a project's outcomes, outside of the direct Solution Delivery Process used by the solution delivery team. We also use the term "Project Environment Participants" to refer to the wide range of people who can influence project outcomes, outside of the direct solution delivery team and commonly identified stakeholders. We use the term "Solution Delivery Capabilities" to describe the wide range of characteristics, both technical and non-technical, exhibited by a Project Environment. This includes characteristics such as on-time delivery, meeting technical performance indicators and cost performance, as well as the ability to innovate, resilience and adaptability. We use this term to emphasize that all these characteristics are the result of management choices made about a Project Environment. This includes choices made on variables which are not traditionally examined as part of an analysis to improve project outcomes, the most fundamental of these being communication.

It is often said that 90 percent of a manager's job is communication. Yet, the communication literature is traditionally couched in the language of soft skills. It doesn't lend itself to the same kind of scientific, analytic management method employed by managers or systems engineers and prescribed by organizations as best practices for Project Performance Management. This book fills that gap. If we spend 90 percent of our time on communication, it makes sense to have a method to figure out if we are spending our time wisely and, if we are not, what we can do to improve communication.

Readership and Benefits

The contents of this book are applicable to leaders as well as people who work on projects, manage projects and those who are responsible for making organizational decisions about Project Environments. To those who work on projects, it will help you understand your environment better so that you can work smarter and more efficiently within your Project Environment. To those who manage projects, it will help you understand your environment better so that you can get more information from the existing environment and improve the performance of your projects. To those responsible for making organizational decisions about Project Environments, it will help you make choices that lead to the type of project outcomes and Solution Delivery Capabilities you want your organization to have. It will also help you design your Project Environments.

The concept of this book is that people produce project outcomes, and communication creates the environment that people work in. The environments we are discussing can be as small as a two-person team and as large as the capability development process used by the US government to discover, develop, acquire and field technology. By focusing on communication, we can improve the way people work. However, this is not a soft skills book; it is a book about applying a scientific method to improving project outcomes.

It follows a scientific approach to learning about an environment: observation, hypothesis, experimentation and conclusion. We can observe communication since so much of it is now done using electronic media that create artifacts. We can analyze the artifacts and observe how people use them. We can then use the results of this analysis and observation to better understand the Project Environment by understanding the communication environment. We apply this approach to the Project Environment to help us learn about the environment so that we can test ways to improve the environment. The goal is to contribute to our knowledge about Project Environments and how they work. The end result is to allow us all, when working on a project, managing a project or designing a Project Environment, to produce the kind of outcomes that make a positive difference in the world.

This book is untraditional in its approach; it takes imagination. But, like the famed Einstein quote,[1] I believe that imagination is "a real factor in scientific research." It asks us to think creatively and broadly about the underlying causes of project performance. It also asks us to think imaginatively about how we can develop rigorous and robust tools to manage project performance using a newfound understanding of what causes project performance. Though the thinking needs to be imaginative, the goal is anything but flighty. The goal of this book is to help people produce better project outcomes and healthier Project Environments.

This book was made possible by my wife. Her unwavering belief in me, through the ups and downs of life as an entrepreneur and independent consultant, is the reason this book exists. I would also like to thank my editor, Jonathan Norman, for his constructive feedback, honest insight and positive delivery of every message. I would like to thank my fellow board members of the College of Performance Management (CPM) and the entire CPM community. It is an unparalleled source of experience, expertise and topical discussions on Project Performance Management. I thank my parents for everything, in the most encompassing and significant sense of literally everything. I thank my in-laws for the many gifts they have bestowed upon me (the most important of which is my wife) and my grandparents for the incredible role they play in my life. To our children, there are no words to describe the breadth and simplicity

---

1   "Imagination is more important than knowledge. For knowledge is limited, whereas imagination embraces the entire world, stimulating progress, giving birth to evolution. It is, strictly speaking, a real factor in scientific research." Albert Einstein, *Einstein on Cosmic Religion and Other Opinions and Aphorisms*. Mineola, NY: Dover Publications, 2009. Originally published in 1931 by Covici-Friede, Inc.

of our dreams for you and the ways in which we are trying to prepare you to attain them. I am humbled by the life I am living. Thank you.

I have had the honor of being associated with many companies, institutions and organizations. The views expressed here are my own.

Glossary

This glossary defines and discusses terms which are newly introduced in the book or which are used in non-traditional ways. It is alphabetical except for the terms related to communication analytics. These are given at the end and are grouped in the order they are presented in the book to provide more relevant context for the terms.

Communication

Communication is the information people receive. It is received through the full range of human senses and sense-making abilities. It includes information that is intentionally generated by a person, such as an e-mail which they send out. It also includes information that is unintentionally generated by a person, such as the way they treat another person and a third party's observation of that treatment. Communication is the input people use to decide how to behave. It is the set of observations people use to learn behaviors and adapt to an environment. As such, communication directly shapes the reality in and of a project environment.

Communication Design

Communication Design is the design of the communication environment. It is the system design of how people communicate, interact and behave.

Communication Design Elements as well as Elements of Communication Design and Design Elements

Elements of Communication Design are observable manifestations of communication design. They reflect the design of the communication environment and include intentional and unintentional actions and decisions.

Communication Environment

The Communication Environment is the structure of an environment as it relates to communication. It determines the communication generated in an environment.

Communication Objects

Communication Objects are the artifacts generated by the process of communication. A communication object is more than the information it is meant to contain; it is made up of numerous elements, including descriptors of the container itself. This is much like how an in-person conversation between two people is made up of non-verbal elements as well as the words in the conversation. Communication Objects encompass the "non-verbal" elements of communication and are a reflection of the design of the communication environment.

Communication Object Elements as well as Elements of Communication Objects and Object Elements

Communication Object elements are the full range of measurable aspects of a communication object and are descriptors of a communication object. They play an important role in how communication objects are used, telling us about the communication environment and the people in the environment. They are generated by applying an analytic tool or method to communication objects.

Observable Manifestations

Observable Manifestations are visible expressions of an underlying structure or process. For example, the structure of a project environment may not be readily apparent. However, the observable phenomena of schedule lateness can be observed. Another example is that the way someone thinks about uncertainty may not be readily apparent. However, the observable phenomena of limiting who a manager can use on a project team can be observed.

OODA as well as the OODA Loop

OODA is an acronym for Observe, Orient, Decide, Act. It is a theory of human behavior proposed by John Boyd.[1] It is used extensively throughout this book as an underlying description explaining human behavior. It proposes that human behavior in an environment can be understood as conforming to a four-stage process: observation of data in an environment, orientation relative to the data and the environment, decision making with respect to the data and the environment, and action within the environment. This process is iterative and is referred to as the OODA Loop.

Performance Management Tool

A Performance Management Tool is a conceptual construct for managing the solution delivery capabilities of a project environment. It identifies the relevant determinants of project performance and the inter-relationship of the determinants. Every performance management tool carries a set of underlying assumptions on the structure of a project environment and people's behavior. These assumptions influence the way we perceive a project and the people involved with the project. As such, a performance management tool implicitly defines the reality of the project and how project participants are managed.

Project

A project is a model for solving problems and accomplishing work. It is a model for organizing people, resources and information. There is a strict definition of a project as "a temporary endeavor undertaken to create a unique product, service, or result."[2] In other words, it is different from operations which are an ongoing activity. However, projects have become a common model for thinking about work and human activity in general. The project model is being widely applied as a way to structure organizations, people and ongoing work efforts. As a result, project management and lessons from managing projects have an increasing applicability to the way in which

---

1   John R. Boyd, "Patterns of Conflict," briefing presentation, December 1986, available at: http://www.ausairpower.net/JRB/poc.pdf.
2   Project Management Institute, *A Guide to the Project Management Body of Knowledge (PMBOK® Guide)*, 5th edn. Newtown Square, PA: Project Management Institute, 2013.

organizations solve problems, accomplish work and produce. Conversely, lessons and tools from other fields that have long been focused on work and human activity are becoming increasingly relevant to thinking about projects and project management. This includes fields of study such as economics, communication, marketing, organizational theory, psychology, sociology and anthropology.

Project Environment

A Project Environment is the broad environment in which the project takes place. It includes direct project factors, such as the people chosen to be part of the project team and the project budget. It also includes broader factors, such as how people are chosen to be part of the project team and the process for obtaining a budget. This definition of a project environment includes broad influences such as institutional context, regulations and culture. It also includes the influence of individuals and organizations that may not be classified as direct project stakeholders in a traditional definition of a project, such as Project Environment Participants.

Project Environment Participants

Project Environment Participants are the wide range of people and groups who can influence project outcomes. It includes traditionally defined participants such as the direct solution delivery team and commonly identified stakeholders, but it expands the definition to include other people and groups that influence project outcomes. For example, the project manager of a US government program may build their project plan without considering the influence of the US Congress. However, the US Congress approves all funds for government projects. If the Congress fails to approve the necessary funds, the program will run into problems regardless of the project manager's project plan.

Project Environment Participants also include people and groups that influence the structure of a project environment. For example, a company's human resources policy determines the people who are available for a project manager to use on their projects. Thus, the human resource department is a participant in the project environment.

Project Performance Management

Project Performance Management is the act of intentionally influencing a project environment to increase the probability of the project environment exhibiting the desired solution delivery capabilities. Traditionally, this has meant creating an expectation of the performance of schedule, budget and work product delivery, and then influencing the project environment so that it meets those expectations.

However, Project Performance Management is not limited to defining performance in those traditional terms; it can include a wide range of performance characteristics and solution delivery capabilities. For example, an environment can be managed to increase the probability of producing innovative, market-leading ideas, encourage creative problem solving and react quickly to changes in the market.

Project Performance Management is always a choice between alternatives. The design choices made about the structure of the project environment influence the range of alternatives available. This, in turn, influences the relative cost and probability of success of pursuing a specific set of performance characteristics and solution delivery capabilities. For example, an environment designed to repurpose commercially available technology in ways that provide a competitive advantage in the market, in order to keep research and development costs low, is far less likely to succeed in delivering market advantage solutions than an environment designed to deliver market advantage solutions using a small research and development budget. The budget numbers may be the same for both, but, because the means of producing the solution are not defined in the second case, the outcomes will likely be different. The second case has a much higher probability of success.

Revealed Preferences

Revealed Preferences is an economic principle that states that we can understand people and their environment by observing the choices they make. The principle of revealed preferences facilitates inferences about decision-making processes and the information used to make those decisions.

Solution Delivery Capabilities

Solution Delivery Capabilities is a description of the solutions that an environment is capable of delivering. The description can be expressed in terms of a domain or boundary such as a software solution. The description can also be expressed in terms of a performance characteristic such as timeliness or innovation. For example, an environment can be described as able to deliver innovative software solutions on time and on budget.

Solution Delivery Process

The Solution Delivery Process is the process or processes by which an environment delivers solutions.

Structure, Structure of the Environment, Structure of the Project Environment, Communication Structure, Structure of the Communication Environment, etc.

Structure is the organizing principle for a specific domain. The Structure of the Project Environment, for example, is how the environment is organized with respect to projects. It can be viewed as a whole or it can be viewed through different lenses which expose a specific aspect of the project environment. For example, the Communication Structure is one lens through which to look at a project environment. It reveals the way the environment is organized with respect to communication in the project environment. It can be further analyzed and viewed through more focused lenses by applying analytic tools to the communication environment or to communication objects in the environment.

Integrated Communication Strategy (ICS) or Communication Strategy

An Integrated Communication Strategy (ICS) is a combination of the decisions consciously taken to design the communication environment. It can include design decisions such as the schedule of communication, the workflow of communication, which methods of communication are used and the rules of using that method. When overlaid on top of a communication schedule, the

ICS creates a time-phased, integrated description of communication activity in the project environment which can then be used to generate and perform communication analytics on the project environment.

Planned Communication (P COM)

Planned Communication (P COM) is the amount of communication planned, or scheduled, to take place over a particular period of time. It is expressed in the unit of measurement of the communication.

Actual Communication (A COM)

Actual Communication (A COM) is the actual amount of communication that took place over a particular period of time. It is expressed in the unit of measurement of the communication.

Communication Variance (COM V)

Communication Variance (COM V) is the variance between actual communication and planned communication for a particular period of time. It is A COM – P COM and is expressed in the unit of measurement of the communication.

Measurable Communication Action (MCA)

A Measurable Communication Action (MCA) is a single unit of measurement of communication in an environment. It provides a means to measure and integrate multiple communication methods, communication elements and design decisions into a single unit of measurement. It can be made up of a single method of communication or multiple methods of communication. The methods can be added together, giving all methods equal weight, or different methods can be weighted when combining them into an MCA. The weighting can reflect variables such as the relative value management places on each form of communication or the strictness with which communication design decisions are enforced for each method of communication. It can reflect the phase of the project or the expected activities for that period of time.

It can be tweaked to increase sensitivity towards one method of communication over another to facilitate management awareness of unpredicted behavior.

Introduction: Communication as a Project Performance Management Tool

This book provides a new way of thinking about communication on a project. It proposes that communication can be a rigorous Performance Management Tool and, further, that managing communication as a Performance Management Tool is essential for delivering desired outcomes. It is essential because all projects are social environments.

General Norman Schwarzkopf tells the story[1] of how he would train new leaders in an armored division. These are the young men and women in charge of tanks. To paraphrase, the story goes something like this. He would bring them to where the tanks were parked.

"Have you studied the manual on how the tank operates?" he would bark.

"Yes! Sir!" would come the reply.

"Are you 100 percent certain that you know how to operate the tank?"

"Yes! Sir!" the trainee would reply.

"Soldier! I would like you to move in front of that tank over there and command it to move." He would order.

"Yes! Sir!" would come the reply.

---

1   I heard it from him at a management seminar in the late 1990s or early 2000s in Dearborn, Michigan.

The recruit would then march in perfect form to in front of the tank. He would drop his arms to his side, face the tank and stop, bewildered.

"Is there a problem, soldier?" the General would ask.

"No! Sir!" would come the reply.

"Well?" ordered the General, "Command the tank to move!"

The recruit wouldn't know what to do. He would stand with a puzzled look on his face, then would do as the General had asked.

"Tank!" said the soldier, "Move!"

The tank wouldn't move. The soldier looked at the General. The General looked unhappy.

"Tank!" shouted the soldier, "MOVE!"

The tank wouldn't move. The General looked even more unhappy. The soldier started to get nervous.

"TANK! I SAID MOVE!" the soldier would command.

The tank wouldn't move.

The General looked at the soldier and shouted, "You said, soldier, that you studied the manual! You said, soldier, that you knew how to operate the tank! You have stood here now for three minutes and the tank has not moved. Is something wrong with my tank? Is my tank broken?! Why isn't my tank moving?!"

"Sir! The tank isn't moving because it is empty, Sir"

"What?"

"There isn't anyone inside to operate the tank, Sir!"

"Oh" the General said. "You mean the tank doesn't work without people?"

"Yes Sir" the recruit would answer.

And the lesson would be over.

It takes people to get things done. A project without people is simply a set of numbers: most often a timeline and budget and buckets of tasks. A project without people is like the tank in the General Schwarzkopf story—it cannot go anywhere without people making it happen. Communication is how we work. Communication is how people share with each other and creates the environment in which people get work done. It is this environment which defines the kind of solutions people can develop. Communication is how we can manage the environment.

Communication shapes people's perceptions and it defines the range of actions someone is willing to take in a Project Environment. John Boyd, the fabled American military strategist and aircraft designer, taught that people take actions as a result of a continuous cycle of observation, orientation, decision making and action. He called this the OODA Loop.[2] We observe our environment and based on our previous experiences, training, previous observations and background, we orient ourselves to the environment, integrating the latest observation into how we make sense of the environment. Based on our orientation and this observation, we make a decision on how to act, then we act.

It's a lot like reading the road when driving. We see a car edging into our lane and try to understand what it's doing. We figure out that it is trying to come into our lane, so we decide that we should let it into the lane. We take action by slowing down and letting it come into our lane.

People receive communications throughout a project lifecycle. The communications they receive are the way they observe the Project Environment. The communications may lead to action, such as the recipient deciding to undertake a particular task, or the recipient may decide not to act, in which case the task is not taken up. Either way, it is started by receiving a communication.

What's more, whether or not the person decides to act is a result of their orientation within the environment. While each person may bring their particular background, experiences and training to a project, eventually, people's orientation within a specific environment becomes influenced by what they see and experience within that environment. In other words,

---

2   John R. Boyd, "Patterns of Conflict," briefing presentation, December 1986. Available at: http://www.ausairpower.net/JRB/poc.pdf.

people learn from their environment and change their behaviors as a result of what they've learned. They learn from how they are treated and how other people are treated. They learn from their observations about themselves in the environment and their observations about others in the environment. It is an iterative cycle, a continuous loop.

We can learn how people react to specific observations about their environment. We can see their behavior in response to receiving a specific observation, such as a specific communication. This gives us insight into their orientation and decision-making process. If someone used to take up a task every time we sent them an e-mail and now they don't, we know something has changed. Their orientation and decision-making process has changed.

We can use the connection between communication and action to manage Project Environments. A vast majority of project communication is done with electronic communication media that produce artifacts. We can observe and analyze these artifacts. We can trace the artifacts and see what people do with them or, at least, how people act once they receive the artifact. This is the starting point of how we can use communication as a Performance Management Tool.

We can apply a range of analytic tools to the artifacts to separate out what element of the artifact connects to what type of behavior. We can also apply simple arithmetic and see whether the quantity of communication leads to a particular pattern of behavior. For example, will sending 10 e-mails to my customer have them get back to me any faster? We can apply more advanced analytic methods such as studying word choice or the emotional tone of an artifact and see whether these make a difference in how people behave. For example, will using technical words and a negative tone in a project report get me signed-off on a change request? There is a wide array of elements we can isolate and connect to people's behavior.

Observing the connection between a communication artifact and a person's behavior helps us understand a person's orientation and decision-making process. We may not be able to get inside somebody's head, but we can better understand how they work by seeing how they act in response to specific communications.

We can take this approach even further and use it to understand the constraints that a communication environment places on people. People will generally act as they are expected to. They learn what is expected of them through observation. They also receive explicit communication on what's expected of them and implicit communication on how to act from observing the environment. They observe how they are treated when they act as expected and they observe how other people are treated.

All of this information on how to act comes from observing and being part of the communication environment. In this way, the communication environment shapes how people act. The information gleaned from the environment may be intentionally conveyed, such as a rule of when you can talk to suppliers when bidding out a project. Alternatively, it may be unintentionally conveyed, such as getting into trouble for talking to an unapproved supplier during the project lifecycle.

This information, whether intentionally conveyed or unintentionally conveyed, shapes the kind of solutions a project delivers. Conway's Law, which we will look at in Chapter 1, says that the solution a project delivers is a direct reflection of the communication environment of the project. That means that the design of the communication environment directly impacts the project's outcome. This is a key connection of how we can use communication to manage project performance.

We will describe different Communication Design choices. These are elements of the Communication Environment that influence how people act. We will use the same approach as we did above, connecting a design element to people's behavior. We can look at simple design choices, such as who you are allowed to assign tasks to. We can see whether changing that element changes how people behave and therefore the solutions they deliver. We can look at more subtle design choices, such as guidelines on how to use e-mail for project reporting. We can see how that design element affects people's behavior and the kinds of solutions they deliver. Observing the connection between a specific Communication Design element and a person's behavior can help us better understand the specific impact of that element on what our projects deliver.

People work together to deliver a project. We can observe the behavior of individuals. We can also observe the behavior of an entire project team. We can then use these observations to draw connections between specific communication elements and how a project team behaves, and use this understanding to manage team behavior using communication.

We will see that team behavior alone does not determine the success of a project. A project operates in an environment full of other stakeholders and external factors that constrain a project. We will argue that these stakeholders and external factors are as important to the success of the project as the behavior of the project team. A perfectly executed project, for example, will fail if the sponsors pull the project's budget.

This observation leads us to a fundamental design element. This element describes the types of problems which an environment is oriented to handle. Most environments are oriented to work with stakeholders and factors within the limited span of control of the manager. This leaves the manager powerless to manage the numerous other variables which could impact their project's performance.

Yet, managers don't have to be powerless with respect to these variables. We can use communication to extend our management of project performance and manage these other variables. Traditional Project Performance Management Tools fail because they seek to bring these variables within the manager's span of control or they seek to wrestle these variables into an existing problem for which the management tool has an answer. This doesn't work because, by definition, these variables are outside of the manager's span of control and, very often, they can't be wrestled into an existing problem.

These variables come from people with different goals operating under different constraints from those of the project. They can't be made to fit into the project; the project has to expand to work with them. This is accomplished through communication. Just as we can use communication to manage people's behavior within the project team, we can also use it to work with people's behavior outside of the project team. This will empower managers and contribute to better solutions. Using communication to manage project performance expands the range of solutions we can deliver and improves our ability to deliver the right solutions.

However, this is not a soft skills book. Part of the rethinking argued here is that we can create knowledge about the impact of communication on project performance in our environments. We can define discrete elements to observe and measure, such as the volume of e-mails sent to a customer and the schedule performance of our projects. We can see if there is any connection between the two. We can better understand what elements to focus on to improve project performance. We can build guidelines and a knowledge base of communication best practices that improve project performance in our environment and we can use that knowledge to manage project performance with communication.

It all boils down to people. Projects are undertaken by people. And all projects are social environments. Communication is how we manage people and social environments. This is critical because people are at the core of today's competitive environment. More so than at almost any time in history, people are empowered to challenge organizations, companies and countries in an entirely new way. Revolutions in communication technologies, such as the Internet, and in usability have opened up near-limitless potential for individuals to create ideas, spread them and implement them. It no longer takes a university, a corporation or a large national enterprise to upset the status quo; this can be done from a smartphone with off-the-shelf technologies in an apartment and spread worldwide.

We address the specific role of people in Part II of this book. People, we will argue, are the source of all uncertainty in a Project Environment. Even technical and budgetary issues can be boiled down to people. The choices people make in a Project Environment are not determinable by a well-defined set of formulae or algorithms. There is no way to predict human behavior in Project Environment. Yet, the traditional tools for designing, executing and managing Project Environments are based on the prediction of human behavior. We are trained to disaggregate a problem into smaller parts, work the problem at a component part level and reintegrate it. This works when the component part can be "worked" toward a single solution. However, when dealing with people, there is no single solution—there are a myriad of solutions whose acceptability depends on human choice. People can choose to accept a potential solution or not.

The traditional method for designing, executing and managing Project Environments can serve us well when we operate in a competitive environment where achieving our goals depends on solving problems that can be worked toward a single solution. However, this is becoming less the case for most competitive organizations. We are operating in an environment driven by empowered people. To achieve our goals, we need to design, execute and manage our Project Environments with the unpredictability of people in mind. Using communication as a Performance Management Tool gives us a deeper understanding of how to approach designing, executing and managing Project Environments so that we can achieve our goals in today's competitive landscape.

This has implications for the way organizations and institutions research, develop, acquire and go to market or deploy new technologies in a competitive landscape, whether a competitive marketspace or a competitive threat environment. The ability to dominate a specific space is increasingly dependent on people, individual creativity and adaptability in a situation, as opposed to the outcome of a fixed, prediction-based process. The traditional processes and problem-solving tools currently used for deciding what to develop, how to develop and how to go to market with new developments constrain individual creativity and adaptability. We need a new tool set for performance management, one that is a better fit for the competitive landscape, if we want to dominate a competitive space. Communication, as a Performance Management Tool, is the right tool set.

How to Use this Book

Here is the general lay of the land for this book. Use this section to plan out what to read.

This book is separated into two parts:

- *Part I*: this part develops the argument for using communication as a Performance Management Tool because communication determines project outcomes and the capabilities of any project environment.

- *Part II*: this part develops the argument for the competitive need to use communication as a Performance Management Tool when designing our project environments because all uncertainty, both within a project environment and across a competitive landscape, comes from people.

Each chapter *introduces a concept and develops the argument* that will be covered within that chapter.

Each chapter uses numerous *examples to illustrate the concepts*. Use the examples to quickly see the argument develop. If you are reading this in electronic format, a search for "example" will quickly guide you toward the examples.

Each chapter has a section on *"What it Means for Us," describing how to use the concept in your everyday work*. It is the application of the concepts. "What it Means for Us" is how the concepts can be used to design and manage project environments that have desired Solution Delivery Capabilities and produce desired outcomes. It deals with design, planning, execution, management and controlling project environments.

Spotlights are concise case studies or discussions of the concepts at play in the real world. They often contain specific lessons and conclusions. If you are looking for the quickest way to get a sense of the book's argument, read these.

Chapters 5 and 6 go into depth on a formal approach for using communication as a Performance Management Tool. It contains numbers, a few formulas, tables and graphs. They are extremely helpful for driving home the point that communication doesn't have to be a soft skills area of management. They also demonstrate how communication can be used in an analytically rigorous and formal environment for performance management. However, numbers and formulas are not for everyone, so consider yourself forewarned.

Wicked uncertainty and its implications for how we design and lead projects that provide competitive advantage are discussed in Chapters 7 and 8. Strategists, executives, product developers and systems designers are directed to the brief *Epilogue* at the end of Chapter 8 where dominance in a competitive space is examined by understanding the role of empowered individuals in creating a hybrid, asymmetric competitive environment. It concludes by proposing that we need to create environments in our organizations that properly unlock the power of people if we want to dominate a competitive space. The Epilogue is the "What it Means for Us" for the whole book, looking beyond the details of the method, to why we need to get our methods and tools right in the long run. If we don't, our organizations may not survive.

The Appendix provides a tangible example of Communication Objects, Communication Object elements and the impact different elements have on the success of an organization meeting its goals. The case study differs in style from the rest of the book and is a story, like an extended Spotlight, focused on an IT Department and a project manager relying on the IT department for her project. Finally, here is my *website and e-mail address* if you want to keep tabs on the latest developments about this subject, keep in touch or ask any questions: www.communicationmeasurement.org and markphillipsconsult@gmail.com.

PART I
Why Communication Matters

1

Communication Determines
Project Outcomes

Research has shown that there is a direct connection between communication and a project's outcome. Specifically, a project's outcome is directly determined by the design of the communication environment of the project.

This theory was proposed by Melvin Conway in 1968 in a *Datamation* magazine article entitled "How Do Committees Invent?" In it, he put forth an idea that has come to be known as Conway's Law. It says that "organizations which design systems (in the broad sense used here) are constrained to produce designs which are copies of the communication structures of these organizations."[1] In other words, the solutions that teams come up with mirror the structure of those teams. There is a *structure-preserving* relationship between the team that works on a project and the project itself. Their shapes match, they mirror each other—or, in technical terms used by Conway, "there is a homomorphism [mirroring] from the linear graph of a system to the linear graph of its design organization."[2] What this means is that the design of the project's communication environment will be mirrored in the project outcome.

For example, a government agency has requirements for a new product. To develop the product, it works with its contracting department and hires a large contractor. The large contractor has two internal development teams and also has relationships with three other subcontractors which it will work with on this project. Conway's Law suggests that the final product will consist of at least five subsystems, reflecting the two internal development teams and the three subcontractors. Further, the interface between the subsystems and the nature of the final product will reflect the effectiveness and quality of the

---

1   Melvin E. Conway, "How Do Committees Invent?", 1968, available at: http://www.melconway.com/research/committees.html.
2   Ibid.

interpersonal communication between all parties including the subcontractors, the internal development teams, the program manager at the large contractor, the government agency and the contracting department.

The mirroring effect described by Conway is supported by empirical research from a Harvard Business School Working Paper.[3] In it, the authors state:

> Specifically, products tend to "mirror" the architectures of the organizations in which they are developed. This dynamic occurs because the organization's governance structures, problem solving routines and communication patterns constrain the space in which it searches for new solutions. Such a relationship is important, given that product architecture has been shown to be an important predictor of product performance, product variety, process flexibility and even the path of industry evolution.

The decisions we make about the communication environment of our teams and the communication processes determine project performance. These decisions are expressed in the communication design. Communication design is how we design the communication environment on our projects. It is the flow of the communication on a project and is the system design of how people communicate and interact. Communication design, as a separate field of study, is based on the awareness that communication is not about reporting on data from a project; rather, it is about shaping reality on a project.

This is a fundamentally different view of communication from that discussed in standard project management texts such as *A Guide to the Project Management Body of Knowledge (PMBOK® Guide)* (4th edn) from the Project Management Institute.[4] This view is radically different from the traditional definition of the role of communication in project management. The traditional approach to a communication plan views the project as an independent endeavor, working on its own, and ignores the impact of system design. In the traditional view, communication is a necessary fluid that runs through the system to keep the wheels turning. The content of communication is determined by the project. People use whatever tools they like, in whatever way they like, to pass along information when they feel they have to. Rather than being a tool for shaping reality and improving project outcomes, communication becomes a burden.

---

3   Alan MacCormack, John Rusnak and Carliss Baldwin, "Exploring the Duality between Product and Organizational Architectures: A Test of the 'Mirroring' Hypothesis," Harvard Business School Working Paper 08-039, 2008.

4   Project Management Institute, *A Guide to the Project Management Body of Knowledge (PMBOK® Guide)*, 4th edn. Newtown Square, PA: Project Management Institute, 2008.

Reluctant project managers and team members ask: what information do I have to send out or pass along now? To me, this explains e-mails forwarded to everyone or a "reply all" with five pages of e-mail back and forth quoted within the e-mail. The sender doesn't realize the power of communication; they are just concerned with getting another task off their plate. E-mail sent. Communication happened. Check.

SPOTLIGHT: THE TRADITIONAL VIEW

Let me tell the story of an exchange I had with a sophisticated, well-paid project manager of complex, large-scale projects. It was following a presentation I'd given about the importance of communication. He stood up at the end of the presentation and flatly denied the importance of paying attention to the details of communication on his projects. He was quite loud and adamant. I asked him if he personally paid attention to all the information that came to him every day. Did he read every e-mail, for example, that he received?

"Of course not" he replied. "I have a filter set up on my e-mail that automatically files any e-mail that I'm cc'd or bcc'd on. I only read e-mails that are sent directly to me."

"Oh" I answered. "And what about the e-mails that you generate? Do you have any rules or guidelines on how you use e-mail to communicate out with others?"

"No! I get to the task of reporting and communication whenever I can. I spend all day on the project! Sometimes I don't get a chance to write reports or e-mails until 3 am. I then write them and send them out." He was proud at his dedication and long hours spent on the project.

"Do you think everybody reads the e-mails that you send at 3 am?" I asked.

He looked at me crossly as an answer.

In his mind, it didn't matter if anyone read them. He had sent out the reports as needed and fulfilled his obligation. (I would further speculate that in his mind he believed that everyone did read the reports since they were sent by him, the project manager.)

With our newfound understanding of the role communication plays, how do you think it makes team members feel when they only hear from their manager in the middle of the night? Do you think they believe he is interested in engaging with them or hearing from them? What do you think a project sponsor's perception is on the status of the project when the manager is sending a report at 3 am? Do you think this gives the impression that things are moving smoothly? With every e-mail and every report, with every communication we have, we have the chance to positively influence the outcome of the project.

Realizing that there is a communication design recognizes that people are responsible for projects and that they are influenced by the information they receive. They use this information to make decisions about the project and how they should act. Whether we are aware of the specific design of our Project Environment or not, as Conway's Law tells us, it directly impacts upon project performance. Here are two case studies showing Conway's Law at work in two major government projects.

Communication Design: A Success Story—The F/A-18 E/F

The F/A-18 E/F Super Hornet program was a $3.3 billion project to develop the upgrade to the F/A-18 fighter jet between 1993 and 2003. It involved a large number of contractors, personnel, stakeholders, managers, etc. There were a lot of moving parts to coordinate and many milestones to reach. The stakeholders were a diverse group that ranged from corporate leadership at large contractors and leadership in the US Navy to elected representatives in the US Congress and the President of the United States. An effort of this size and complexity can be fraught with failure, miscues, waste and distrust.

Instead, the F/A-18 E/F Super Hornet program is considered to be a definitive success.[5] It came in on budget, on time and even over-delivered on technical performance metrics (the plane was 400 lbs lighter than anticipated). It also has an impressive record from a process implementation standpoint. The initial estimates about cost and schedule that were made at the beginning of the project using Earned Value Management (EVM) were proven to be a valuable management tool 10 years later. This speaks volumes of the strengths of performance management done right and the skill of the program management team.

I had the chance to learn more about the secret to the program's success at a workshop with a panel of key program leaders.[6] Each of the panelists echoed

---

5   "The F/A-18 E/F acquisition program was an unparalleled success. The aircraft emerged from Engineering and Manufacturing Development meeting all of its performance requirements on cost, on schedule and 400 pounds under weight. All of this was verified in Operational Verification testing, the final exam, passing with flying colors receiving the highest possible endorsement." United States Navy Fact File, http://www.navy.mil/navydata/fact_display.asp ?cid=1100&tid=1200&ct=1.

6   The panel took place at the 2012 International Integrated Program Management Conference (IPMC) in Bethesda, Maryland on 10 December 2012. It was comprised of Mr Gary Bliss, SES, the director of one of two offices responsible for cost estimates of Major Defense Acquisition Programs including the F/A-18 E/F, Vice Admiral (US Navy, Retired) Joseph Dyer, the F/A-18

the same theme: trust, which was named the single biggest contributor to the success of the program. There was trust among and between the stakeholders, the team members, industry, the military and the government. To paraphrase Vice Admiral Dyer, the program manager, "we got the big things right, up front" and that was: creating trust. This trust started in the planning phase of the project and continued throughout the program for over 10 years.

But trust doesn't happen by itself, particularly in a massive, complex, politically approved project. This trust is built and maintained through communication design. (The communication was so effective, joked the Vice Admiral, that it held up his receiving of his first star because his communication strategy was the subject of an internal security investigation.) Leadership designed the environment by setting the rules for communication and modeling behavior. They set a tone for truth in communication and sharing that truth with everyone involved. The members of the team were all playing in the same ballpark with the same reality. And the rules were clear, consistent and applied to everyone.

They adopted the rule that project information would be conveyed using EVM data. Therefore, the data had to be accurate and reliable. Next, they made sure to look at the data and then they distributed it to keep everyone on the same page. The EVM data was looked at on a weekly basis, reviewed with the program team on a weekly basis and shared with key stakeholders. Decisions were made based on that data and the reasons behind decisions were clearly understood by everyone because of this. Decisions could be reasonably predicted because everyone had the same data and the same goal. This created an atmosphere of trust and transparency in communications. Personal agendas, politics and biases played second fiddle to the importance of the performance management data which reflected the reality of the project's movement toward achieving the technical, budgetary and schedule goals of the project.

Following Conway's Law, this design had several implications. First, the team members and stakeholders could focus on advancing the projects goals in a way that would be reflected in the performance management data. Whatever they did had to move the needle, as it were, of the EVM data. Second, the team members and stakeholders could focus solely on advancing the project's goals.

Program Manager, and Mr James Lackey, SES, who was the team leader for the program. The panel was moderated by Mr Wayne Abba, who was the senior analyst for the Office of the Secretary of Defense analyzing Major Defense Acquisition Programs, including the F/A-18 E/F. See the following link for more information: http://ipmconference.org/wp-content/uploads/2012/06/New-WS-02-FA-18EF-Workshop-Leadership-in-Acquisition_v1.pdf.

Leadership provided the necessary cover and political protection to allow them to concentrate on their work as long as it was in the service of the overall project. This had the further effect of facilitating open dialogue among team members and stakeholders since everyone was evaluated based on the overall progress of the project. Leadership successfully integrated and unified the motivation and efforts of disparate groups toward the achievement of the project's goals. The solution that was developed and delivered did the same thing. It is a complex piece of equipment, with numerous disparate parts and systems that are all successfully integrated into a single fighter jet that effectively meets its goals.[7]

Communication Design: A Failure—the Mars Climate Orbiter

The $193 million Mars Climate Orbiter disintegrated upon entering the Martian atmosphere on 23 September 1999 because of poor communication design.

The onboard flight system software for the Orbiter in the Martian atmosphere generated data in imperial units. The software on the ground, back on earth, was written to utilize and send instructions in metric units.[8] There was a lack of a common language between the systems and no integration effort ahead of time that could have caught this error. The preliminary report on the cause of the problem acknowledges the role played by the design of the process in how the disparate systems were developed, integrated and deployed.[9] "People sometimes make errors" said Dr Edward Weiler, NASA's Associate Administrator for Space Science. "The problem here was not the error, it was the failure of NASA's systems engineering, and *the checks and balances in our processes* [emphasis added] to detect the error. That's why we lost the spacecraft." "Our inability to recognize and correct this simple error has had major implications" said Dr Edward Stone, Director of the Jet Propulsion Laboratory.

The scientists involved were all capable of recognizing and correcting the error had there been an opportunity to do so in the Project Environment. The design of the Project Environment did the opposite; it allowed a simple error to be hidden and therefore uncorrected, with disastrous consequences for the project.

---

7   US Department of Defense, Selected Acquisition Report RCS: DD-A&T(Q&A)823-549, F/A-18 E/F, 31 December 2011.
8   NASA, "Mars Climate Orbiter, Mishap Investigation Board Phase I Report," 10 November 1999.
9   NASA, "Mars Climate Orbiter Team Finds Likely Cause of Loss," 30 September 1999, http:// mars.jpl.nasa.gov/msp98/news/mco990930.html.

What it Means for Us

Conway's Law has significant implications. It means that the solution that our teams come up with depends on how we structure the communications on the team. It means that part of our role involves designing the communication environment on a project. We are communication designers. As managers, the way we design and create the communication environment directly impacts the project. To quote Conway: "We have found a criterion for the structuring of design organizations: a design effort should be organized according to the need for communication."[10] We can optimize the Project Environment to meet the project's goals by changing the communication environment of the project.

Even in cases where we don't have full control over the project's communication environment, being aware of it adds to the list of places where we should look for the root cause of problems on a project and where we can look to find solutions. If we ignore the communication environment, we are making a choice to accept it for what it is and are agreeing to manage the project under constraints that may or may not help it. If we pay attention to the communication environment, even if we cannot change it, we can consciously manage the project within the constraints, tweaking the items we do have control over so that we can meet our goals while working within the constraints. We can tailor our communication and what we communicate to increase its effectiveness within the communication environment, and we can improve our ability to contribute to the project and increase our value to project participants.

---

10 Conway, "How Do Committees Invent?"

2

Elements of Communication Design

Communication Design is how we design the communication environment. These are the actions and decisions that affect the communication environment and, consequently, the outcome of projects. The solution delivered by project participants reflects the communication environment. Here is a list of common design elements of a communication environment.

Design Elements of a Communication Environment
➢ Organizing Teams
➢ Locating Teams
➢ Assigning Tasks
➢ Describing Task Information
➢ Coordinating Activity
➢ Who Can Talk to Who in a Project Environment
➢ Defining the Methods of Communication
➢ Setting Rules for Each Method
➢ Defining the Method for Specific Subject-Matter Domains
➢ The Schedule of Communication
➢ The Workflow of Communication
➢ Integrated Communication Strategy

Organizing Teams

The way you organize the project delivery team is a Communication Design decision. As Conway says: "Given any design team organization, there is a class of design alternatives which cannot be effectively pursued by such an organization because the necessary communication paths do not exist."[1] Decisions include whether it is a small team of a few people or a large team

---

1   Conway, "How Do Committees Invent?"

comprised of different companies, subcontractors and agencies. How will the team members communicate with each other and how often? Do they have to go through an intermediary? Are people grouped by functional specialty, e.g. a group of user experience designers on one team and a group of engineers on another, or are the teams cross-functional? These are traditional decisions made on projects. However, they are usually made without regard to the impact that these decisions, as Communication Design decisions, have on the project outcome.

As we saw in Chapter 1 with the F/A-18 and the Mars Climate Orbiter, the products delivered directly reflected the structure of the communication environment. The Communication Design decisions made on how people were grouped into teams, what was communicated and how they communicated across the project were mirrored in the final products.

Locating Teams

Where teams are located affects how often they can communicate and how they will communicate, i.e. what tools they will use to communicate with each other and whether there will be informal interactions. Consequently, locating teams is a Communication Design decision. Are all interface designers on one floor and all the electrical engineers on another? Are the financial analysts located in a different country from the software developers on a project? Are the account managers in the same office as the project managers? These decisions determine constraints on the communication environment of the project.

For example, locating a customer support helpdesk in a different country from the product developers constrains communication between the customer and the product developers. In order to communicate customer experiences from the support team to the product developers, processes and software need to be implemented that capture and convey customer feedback. This adds an additional level of complication and potential miscommunication between the customer and the product developers. The limitations of the additional processes and software will be reflected in the product development decisions made and ultimately in the next version of the product.

Further, locating customer support in a different country from the product developers constrains the transfer of knowledge between product development and customer support. Instead of having the option for organic and unplanned back and forth between the development team, which has deep knowledge of the product, and the customer support team, which need that knowledge, the organization has to rely on pre-defined formal processes for knowledge transfer and on knowledge capture/knowledge discovery software. The limitations of these additional processes and software will be reflected in the customer's experience when interacting with customer support and in the ability of customer support to provide an appealing support experience to the customer. The constraint between customer support and product development is reflected in the experience of the customer and the support team. Try as they might, customer support may struggle to provide an appealing experience. The customer can feel that they are being moved through a formal set of pre-defined processes as the support person works through a knowledge discovery/knowledge delivery system.

Assigning Tasks

Your choice of who you assign tasks to is a Communication Design decision. "Every time a delegation is made and somebody's scope of inquiry is narrowed, the class of design alternatives which can be effectively pursued is also narrowed."[2] Possible options fall off the table. For example, if you are having a revenue problem and you assign IT to the problem, they will likely come up with a software solution such as recommending new customer relationship management (CRM) software. Solutions become limited by the limits of the group assigned to that task and the limits on their ability to communicate with other teams.

Describing Task Information

The artifacts we choose to use to describe the work that needs to be done is a Communication Design decision. We use many different artifacts to describe task information, such as requirements documentation, work package descriptions, the work breakdown structure (WBS) itself, a performance management baseline (PMB) and the project schedule. Different team members interpret these artifacts differently. The artifacts we present to each project participant contribute to their perception of what we expect from them. Tailoring the artifacts enables each person to do their job without distraction.

---

2   Ibid.

For example, the information needed from a schedule is not the same for a project sponsor and a member of the project delivery team. A project sponsor looks at the schedule for a record of dates by which project milestones are expected to be completed; they don't need details and descriptions on every work package and task. Presenting them with that information may convey that you don't understand their role and you don't respect their time since you are giving them more information to sift through to get to what they want. In addition, it can lead to the assumption that they have looked at every detail, understood it and approved of it when, on the contrary, they are simply extracting the information they need from it. On the other hand, a member of the project delivery team looks at the schedule as a list of due dates for their specific tasks and descriptions on the work packages they will be working on. Providing them with a high-level list of milestone due dates may be insufficient information for them to get their work done.

SPOTLIGHT: FORMATTING INFORMATION FOR ENGINEERS VERSUS MBAS

The format of task information is a Communication Design decision. People from different professions utilize different formats of information to make decisions. People's decision making improves when they are presented with a format more akin to that which they are used to based on their professional background.

Professor Mario Vanhoucke from the University of Ghent and a PhD student of his conducted an informal study that highlights this phenomenon. He ran a project simulation and presented different groups of students with information on that project, asking them to make a decision on the next steps for the project based on the information they were presented with. If they made the right decision, the project would come in on time; if they made the wrong decision, the project would be late.

He had two different groups of students: engineering students and business school students. He also had two different formats for the same information. One format expressed the information in numbers, while the other expressed the information in a graphical form.

When he presented the engineering students with numerical information, they tended to make the right decision. When he presented the business school students with the numerical information, they underperformed compared to the engineering students in their decision making. However, when he presented the business school students with the graphical information, they performed on a par with the engineering students who received numerical information.

Coordinating Activity

How you choose to coordinate activities across the project is a Communication Design decision. You can choose to have teams continuously coordinate with each other or can do so at pre-defined milestones. You may choose to have them interact directly or through a coordinator. *The Guide to the Project Management Body of Knowledge* (4th edn) calls this the Integration Process. Conway says: "Coordination among the task groups ... provides the only possibility that the separate task groups will be able to consolidate their efforts in a unified system design."[3] Whatever you call it, how you structure coordination has an impact on the project outcome. For example, the failure of the Mars Orbiter could have been avoided if the Communication Design of the Project Environment had allowed the two teams to coordinate the relevant technical information with each other earlier.

Who Can Talk to Whom in a Project Environment

Deciding who can talk to whom on a project is a Communication Design decision. Some Project Environments allow for a free flow of information at all times. Other environments define specific points when project team members and stakeholders can talk to each other. Still other environments leave it up to the relationships that individual stakeholders have with each other. These decisions shape the communication environment on a project and impact project outcomes.

There are numerous variables at play when decisions are made as to who can talk to who in a Project Environment and when. These include conforming to an organizational hierarchy, working within a structure of pre-defined interfaces between organizations, managing the amount of time people can spend talking with each other versus working, concern over managing specific information that may be revealed in conversations and creating an environment that meets non-project goals. For example, in aspiring to create an equal playing field when bidding out work from a municipal government, the procurement office tightly defines when conversations can occur between municipal officials and potential bidders.

These variables impact the structure of the communication environment and, since the structure of the communication environment is mirrored in

---

3   Ibid.

the solution delivered, can have unintended consequences for the solution delivered. For example, the US Department of Defense has established detailed rules governing the disclosure of information during the acquisition process with the goal of increasing competition in order to reduce costs. These rules define when and how bidders can communicate with a potential acquirer, when and how bidders can talk to potential users, and when and how acquisition personnel can communicate with potential bidders or with the public as a whole. The intention is to reduce costs through increased competition by providing a level playing field for information; however, it can have the unintended consequence of enshrining the informational advantage of existing suppliers, thereby reducing competitiveness and failing to reduce costs.

This unintended consequence is a direct result of the limitations built into the communication structure. Tight controls on communication result in limited access to information. This provides an asymmetrical informational advantage to those who can obtain the information through other means and therefore increases the incentive for people to seek information through such means. It also raises the incentive to control access to informal channels that could provide this information. These factors, in turn, restrict competition and alleviate potential pressure to reduce costs. This limited range of potential solutions from a limited number of potential suppliers is a direct result of the constraints in the communication environment.

Defining the Methods of Communication

People can communicate with each other in a number of different ways in a Project Environment. These range from pre-set communication settings like meetings to informal conversations in the hallway. Communication can be conducted in person, over the phone, using video conferencing or through e-mail, chat, wikis, message boards, etc. Defining what ways are available for communication is a design decision that will be reflected in the solution delivered by the project team.

For example, some environments limit communication between sponsors and the project delivery team to e-mail. Conversations in this environment are constrained by the characteristics of e-mail. These include the fact that it generates a permanent record of the conversation and that it can be shared without the sender's permission. These characteristics facilitate oversight of the project and create an environment of care when crafting e-mails. Participants may take these constraints into consideration and generate communication that fits within these constraints. E-mails would therefore either be murky enough to allow for multiple interpretations or conservative in the ideas presented. The solutions delivered by the team will reflect this constraint and will either miss the mark or be cautious iterations of existing solutions.

Setting Rules for Each Method

The rules for how people use the available ways to communicate are a design decision. Managers can let people communicate however they would like or they can create guidelines on how people should use the available means of communication. The decision to provide guidelines or not is a design decision that affects the solution delivered.

For example, meetings can be ad-hoc gatherings whose format, content and outcome are determined by the individual who called the meeting and not according to pre-defined guidelines. Alternatively, guidelines can be created that govern the format, agenda requirements, time allocation, outcome and expected follow-on documents from meetings. Project Environments where a majority of the meetings are ad-hoc structures produce different solutions from Project Environments that have formalized meeting structures.

The substance of the guidelines for communicating also has an impact on the solutions delivered. For example, the guidelines for the short, daily stand-up meetings used by SCRUM Agile project management practitioners are aligned with the rapid development and frequent delivery of solutions that can be incrementally re-developed. The guidelines for long, multi-day strategic planning sessions, on the other hand, are aligned with the cautious development and careful delivery of solutions that are not meant to be re-developed for a long time.

Defining the Method for Specific Subject-Matter Domains

Defining the appropriate content for each communication tool used in a Project Environment is a Communication Design decision. You can set guidelines over what is appropriate content for each tool. This includes guidelines for what are acceptable questions, acceptable answers and acceptable conversations for a specific tool. For example, you can set a guideline that e-mail is the right tool to use for distributing and discussing project reports with recipients, but that questions and answers about specific task information should be reserved for a project wiki. Discussions on requirements or use cases may be reserved for meetings. Defining the appropriate content for each tool clarifies where people should conduct specific types of conversations and subsequently where they should search for previous project-related information on those conversations. This provides clarity and efficiency in the communication environment and is reflected in the solution delivery capabilities of that Project Environment.

Take, for example, an organization that defines that all customer-related interactions be conducted using sales force automation software and that all interactions be recorded in the software according to a consistent set of data entry rules. People in that organization know exactly where to go to get information about meeting a customer's needs and what those needs are. They know what has been tried before and what has made the customer happy. They can rapidly plan on how to meet customer needs and begin working more quickly to meet those needs. People across different departments and from different managers can work together with the information because the way in which it is entered and the terminology used for customer interactions are consistent across the organization. Further, management can get visibility into the organization's ability to meet customer needs, since all efforts related to meeting customer needs are consolidated in a single location with a consistent set of rules on how information is entered and used. This allows management to further tweak the solution delivery process for that Project Environment.

Contrast this with an organization where customer information and records of customer interaction are spread out across various tools without any consistent set of rules on how information is entered. Some information may be in a salesperson's contact list, other information in an e-mail chain with the customer and yet other information in a specification document on a shared drive in the IT department. People in this type of organization will have a more difficult time understanding what the customer's needs are. It will take time to piece together all the information. In addition, it will be harder for people from different departments to work together, since understanding and planning for the customer's needs are dependent on getting a clear and consistent understanding of those needs from each person who recorded part of the information or had some interaction with the customer. Further, management must use different techniques in this organization to tweak and improve the solution delivery process, since it relies on individuals and their individual approaches rather than the execution of a process.

SPOTLIGHT: GETTING VALUABLE SOLUTIONS FROM AN ONLINE QUESTION AND ANSWER SITE

The online question and answer site http://pm.stackexchange.com is a good example of the relationship between defining appropriate content and delivering valuable solutions. The website is focused on answering questions about project management. It is a community-moderated site where anyone can ask a question and anyone can answer a question. Solutions that meet the questioner's needs are voted up, which confers reputation points to the person who wrote the answer. Thus, there is a direct relationship between reputation and the quality of solutions provided. The more people with high reputations means that there are more people who are providing solutions that meet questioners' needs.

Over the course of one year (2012), the site's moderators focused on more tightly defining what is and is not appropriate content for the site. The type of interactions permitted did not have to be defined, since it is specifically a question and answer site and not a chat board or message board. However, the moderators did publish guidelines that could be used to edit people's interactions on the site to make sure that the desired question and answer format was being maintained. This same approach of publishing guidelines was used to make sure that the appropriate content was being generated on the site.

Over that time, the site experienced a 62 percent increase in the number of people who provided quality answers. This reflects an increase in the total number of quality answers. It is driven by an increase in the number of people providing quality answers and the number of quality answers provided by each person. Figure 2.1 shows the correlation between an increase in defining and enforcing what is appropriate content for the site, and the increase in the number of people providing quality answers. The Communication Design decision of defining what is appropriate content for this specific tool led to an increase in the community providing quality solutions to questioners' needs and thus increased the value of the site as a tool.

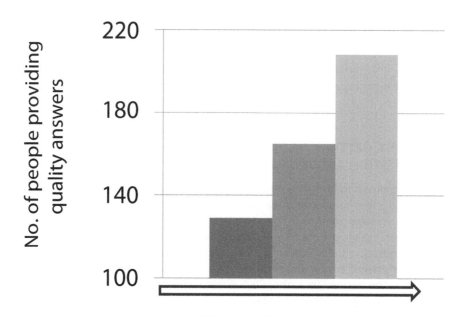

Figure 2.1   Increasing Definition Improves Outcomes
Source: © 2012 Mark Phillips, PMP.

The Schedule of Communication

The schedule of communication can be defined ahead of time. Here is a sample schedule for communication about tasks worked on by a project delivery team:

✓ Updated tasks for a project are sent out on the first Monday of the month.

✓ Questions about the tasks must be submitted by Friday morning of that week.

✓ Responses to the questions are sent out by the following Thursday.

✓   If there are further questions, they are addressed the day after the above step, Friday.

✓   If there are still questions, the task is pushed off for the following month's updated list while the project manager obtains the necessary information to answer the questions.

The schedule of communication directly impacts the project schedule. For example, if we take the sample schedule above, the earliest start date for a task would be the afternoon of the first Friday of the month. That start date is possible only if there aren't any questions about the tasks that are sent out. Assuming that people conform to the communication schedule, the first Friday is when we would know that there aren't any questions. However, if there are questions, that start date would not be possible within the defined communication schedule—either the start date has to shift or the communication schedule needs to be modified.

The Workflow of Communication

The schedule can be combined with specific rules on who talks to who to create a workflow of communication:

✓   Updated tasks for a project are sent out by the project manager on the first Monday of the month to the team leader.

✓   The team leader then distributes tasks out to the team members by Tuesday morning.

✓   The team members should achieve clarification on the tasks amongst themselves.

✓   If questions still remain, team members must submit all questions by Friday morning.

✓   The team leader must send out a single response to all questions by the following Thursday directly to the team member who asked it. If the team leader doesn't know the answer to the questions, they should get answers from the project manager on Tuesday.

✓   If team members still have questions, they should be addressed by the team leader and the project manager on that Friday.

✓   If there are questions that the project manager cannot answer, the task is pushed off for the following month's updated list while the project manager obtains the necessary information.

The specific rules often come from an organization chart. While most people don't think about an organization chart in that way, it defines communication channels. By defining the communication channels, it is part of the Communication Design of the environment and therefore helps to determine the outcome of the solution delivered.

The workflow of communication directly impacts the schedule and the project deliverable, as well as the dynamic between project participants. It can be aligned with the structure of an organizational chart or a pre-defined relationship among participants (such as the relationship between contractors and subcontractors), or it can be unique to a specific project. The communication workflow can either enforce or provide an alternative to existing structures among project participants. The desirability of alignment with existing structures depends on a number of variables, including how well the existing structures perform in meeting the organization's goals and whether the existing structures are the right model to deliver the desired project outcomes for the current project.

Integrated Communication Strategy

The schedule and workflow can be combined with other Communication Design decisions, such as which methods to use, rules on that method and which methods to use for a specific domain to create an Integrated Communication Strategy (ICS). All of these decisions combine to form the communication environment. The decisions you consciously take to design the communication environment form your communication strategy for the project.

The communication strategy integrates the defined methods that people are supposed to use to communicate in the Project Environment with the decision on who can talk to who in the Project Environment. It overlays this information on top of the communication schedule for a time-phased, integrated description of communication activity in the Project Environment.

Here is a sample communication strategy for tasks on a project:

✓ Updated tasks for a project are sent out by the project manager on the first Monday of the month to the team leader.

✓ The team leader then distributes tasks out to the team members by Tuesday morning, with each team member receiving one e-mail to them that contains all the task information. No-one else is cc'd or bcc'd into these e-mails.

✓ The team members should use chat or ad-hoc conversations between themselves to get further clarification on the tasks. However, they should not forward e-mails to each other with the task information and questions.

✓ If questions still remain, the team members must submit all questions by Friday morning; all questions must be in one e-mail sent directly to the team leader without any cc's or bcc's.

✓ The team leader must send out a single response to all questions by the following Thursday directly to the team member who asked it. If the team leader doesn't know the answer to the questions, they should call the project manager on Tuesday for a detailed question and answer session conducted over the phone.

✓ If team members still have questions, a meeting should take place on that Friday with the team members that have questions, the team leader and the project manager. No notes need to be generated from the meeting. The outcome is the project team having sufficient information to work on the tasks.

✓ If there are questions that the project manager cannot answer, the task is pushed off for the following month's updated list while the project manager obtains the necessary information.

This ICS constrains how quickly a project can progress, how quickly changes can be implemented into the solution delivery process, how quickly customer feedback will flow to the project delivery team, and the flow of information between the project delivery team and the customer. It creates an organizational structure where the team is expected to answer their own questions first, without need to record the information or process anywhere (though the option exists to create artifacts if chat is used). In doing so, it leaves the substance of the answers to any questions within the team. Knowledge of who had the question and the dynamic of answering those questions are also left within the team.

This ICS provides clarity to the entire process of solution delivery and the flow of information between the customer and the project delivery team. It defines when, where and how information flows. It also defines where we can look to see where a breakdown happened, since e-mail creates its own artifact, or which artifacts were particularly helpful. We can study the artifacts to see what made them effective or gauge the effectiveness of the entire process to see if it is giving us the desired project outcomes. Do we need to increase the frequency of e-mails or remove the restriction on putting all information into one e-mail? Should we allow for more direct conversations between the project manager and the team members? Should the customer be brought into the process? All of these are valid questions to ask if we are not attaining our desired project outcomes. And all of these are the right questions to ask when we understand the direct connection between Communication Design and project outcomes.

What it Means for Us

An ICS reveals the assumptions we are making of how people work together in a Project Environment. It helps us to understand the underlying operating assumptions of the environment related to people in the environment. It explicitly spells out how people are supposed to get information, communicate information, get knowledge and create knowledge. It also highlights our assumptions of how people are supposed to work together to deliver desired outcomes.

Creating an ICS allows us to check our planned delivery capabilities against the operating assumptions about the people in an environment who have an impact on delivery. For example, using the sample ICS above, let's look at the scenario when the project schedule has a task with a due date of the second Monday of the month. Remember, the task information was sent to the delivery team on the previous Tuesday. Assuming the task requires three days' worth of work, the person who built the project schedule thought it reasonable to achieve a due date of that Friday.

The delivery schedule, however, doesn't take into account the communication flow that people need to complete the task. Meeting a Monday deadline requires the project delivery team not to have any questions about the task that they cannot answer themselves. The Monday deadline precludes the delivery team from asking or answering questions outside of themselves in the method prescribed by the ICS. Thus, if a Monday delivery is required, the ICS needs to change or we need to push back on the delivery schedule.

There is a direct relationship between the design decisions that are behind an ICS and specific project delivery capabilities, such as rapid turnaround in the scenario we are discussing. Were rapid turnaround a desired capability, the ICS needs to change to accommodate this capability. For example, we could shorten the time from receiving information about a task and asking questions outside of the delivery team. We could change the methods the delivery team can use to ask questions of the team leader or even the project manager. An example would be having an in-person meeting with the team leader and the project manager on Wednesday morning, the day after the delivery team received the task information.

Alternatively, we could achieve rapid turnaround by changing the type of tasks that are sent out. For example, we could have the delivery team only work on tasks which they know about and which do not require further explanation. We could select tasks that we know they can answer questions about among themselves. Alternatively, we can forgo a measure of pre-defined parameters for how the task gets done and accept whatever solution the team produces, regardless of any pre-defined parameters. Thus, by controlling the type of work we ask them to perform or accepting a potential range of solutions that they could deliver, we can achieve our desired capability of rapid turnaround.

The ICS makes the underlying operating assumptions explicit and allows us to check our projects against those assumptions. If we don't spell out an ICS, we risk missing out on the opportunity to improve a process that is implicitly taking place in every Project Environment. In every Project Environment, people receive information through communication, ask questions, get further information, create knowledge, make assumptions about information and communicate with each other—it is how people work together to deliver outcomes. By making it explicit, we can design and manage our Project Environments. We can also increase the probability of our environments having specific delivery capabilities and achieving desired outcomes.

When the task delivery schedule is not in concert with the ICS, it means there is a disconnect between the assumptions we are using to create our delivery schedule and the operating assumptions about how people work together to deliver. The disconnect may be intentional or it could reflect a difference in understanding the people in the environment. There could also be other reasons for this. However, we would never know that people were not in concert if we didn't create and compare the task delivery schedule against the ICS. Having the two documents provides us with an opportunity to check our assumptions, spot potential disconnects and point us in the right direction for resolving these disconnects.

The potential for friction in a Project Environment increases when people are operating under different assumptions. It impacts expectations and interpersonal dynamics in the environment. These variables in turn impact the kind of solutions that the environment can deliver. These variables also impact the methods that can be used to deliver desired outcomes, the management techniques available to manage the environment, the resources required to deliver outcomes and the costs involved. Communication can be used as a Performance Management Tool to provide indicators of Project Environment behaviors before they manifest themselves in more traditional ways, such as cost, schedule and technical performance. By using communication as a Performance Management Tool, we can check the consistency of operating assumptions well ahead of potential impacts on cost, schedule and technical performance. Communication as a Performance Management Tool provides insight into the people side of the Project Environment and the social dynamics at work.

While we have been discussing the benefits of creating and working with an ICS, many of the same benefits can be obtained by focusing on a smaller set of design decision elements or even one element. By explicitly recognizing the elements of Communication Design in our Project Environments, we can better understand the factors that impact our solution delivery capabilities.

Later on, we will discuss how an ICS can be combined with measurements of communication to help us analyze our projects as they are being executed and manage the projects to improve outcomes.

To conclude this chapter, remember, it is people operating in the social environment of a project that produce project outcomes. Communication is how people work together. The communication environment is made up of a set of Communication Design decisions about how people communicate and therefore how people work together. Every Project Environment has a communication environment, regardless of whether it is intentionally designed or not. It exists and, as Conway's Law states, it directly impacts project outcomes and project delivery capabilities. By explicitly recognizing the design elements of our communication environment, we can improve project outcomes and design environments that are more likely to exhibit desired solution delivery capabilities.

3

Communication Objects and Communication Design

Communication Design determines the Communication Objects created and used in a Communication Environment. These objects are the artifacts generated by the processes of communication. For example, an environment that allows for e-mail, chat and meetings will generate e-mails, chat logs and minutes from meetings as artifacts. These are the Communication Objects of that Communication Environment and are a direct function of the Communication Environment. You wouldn't expect to receive a Facebook message about the project in the example above; it is not part of the Communication Environment.

By studying Communication Objects, we can learn about the Communication Environment. The objects are a reflection of the design of the Communication Environment. If we did see a Facebook message about the project in the above example, we would know that communication on the project is not conforming to the intended design. We could then investigate as to why that is: what is it about the design, the message sent, the sender or receiver that resulted in a Facebook message being generated instead of an e-mail, chat or a meeting? The Communication Objects in an environment are a rich source of data about the Communication Design. Since Communication Design determines project outcomes, Communication Objects can tell us about the solution delivery capabilities of an environment and its ability to produce desired outcomes.

A Communication Object, though, is different from a traditional project artifact. Project artifacts are generally thought of as the intentional output of a project process. For example, a requirements document is generally considered a project artifact, as is a project charter, scope document, risk register and responsibility matrix. These are all outputs of a project process. The definition of a Communication Object expands on the traditional view and includes items such as e-mails and chats, along with other artifacts created by communication processes.

Further, a Communication Object is more than the information it is meant to contain. It is made up of numerous elements, including descriptors of the container itself, much like how an in-person conversation between two people is made up of non-verbal elements as well as the words in the conversation—there are elements such as body language, dress and how much noise there is in the room where the conversation is taking place—or how an in-person presentation is made up of more than the content in the slides—there are elements such as the presenter's skill as a speaker, the clothes they are wearing, the design of the slides and even the time of day (whether it is before or after lunch, for example), the number of people in the room, how many other presentations the audience has seen that day and the temperature of the room. In the case of Communication Objects created by electronic media such as e-mail, there are elements such as the time of day that the e-mail is sent, how many e-mails the sender sends, how many e-mails the receiver receives, the length of the e-mail and its level of detail.

The information contained in the Communication Object is often only a small part of the communication going on in a Communication Environment. For example, in an in-person conversation, non-verbal elements, such as body language, are estimated to make up 50–80 percent of the message. When we decide whether to believe someone's feelings or not, their words count for only seven percent of our decision, their voice counts for 38 percent and their appearance counts for 55 percent.[1] Accordingly, the content only counts for 7 percent of what the listener factors in when making a decision about what the person is saying. A total of 93 percent of what the listener considers important is non-content-related. As we will see below, the non-content elements of electronically created Communication Objects like e-mail are significant factors.

Yet, despite being only one part of communication, we tend to focus on content when we think about communication. Take, for example, US Defense Acquisition Regulation guidelines regarding project reporting. The guidelines are focused on the content of what needs to be reported—they don't focus on the impact which the process of putting together the content may have on the Project Environment. Another example is the manager in the spotlight in

---

1   Research by Albert Mehrabian, published in many places including Albert Mehrabian, *Silent Messages: Implicit Communication of Emotions and Attitudes,* 2nd edn. Belmont, CA: Wadsworth, 1981. See also http://www.kaaj.com/psych/smorder.html.

Chapter 2 who sends his e-mails at 3 am. He is focused on making sure he sends out the information he believes is necessary; he is not focused on the time of day he sends the message.

Elements of Communication Objects

Communication Object elements are the various non-content portions of the communication and are descriptors of the non-content portions of communication. They play an important role in how Communication Objects are used, tell us about the Communication Environment and the people in the environment. The following are examples of Communication Object elements.

Elements of Communication Objects
➢ Time of Day
➢ Day of the Week
➢ How Much You Broadcast to an Audience
➢ Readability, Word Choice and Emotional Tone
➢ Audience Characteristics
➢ Total Quantity of Information a Person Receives
➢ Boundaries between Groups
➢ Is it a Boundary Object?
➢ The Process that Generates the Communication Object

Communication Object elements are a rich source of data. They can be connected to the behavior of people who receive the Communication Object. As such, we can use the study of Communication Object elements to isolate and identify elements that are correlated with the types of behaviors we want to see from the people in our Project Environment and that we want to see exhibited by our Project Environment as a whole. Here are a few examples of the connection between Communication Object elements and people's behavior. The examples are divided up by Communication Object elements.

Time of Day

One Communication Object element that impacts people's behavior is the time of day that they receive the Communication Object. Dan Zarella[2] studied

---

2   Dan Zarella, *Zarella's Hierarchy of Contagiousness: The Science, Design and Engineering of Contagious Ideas*. The Domino Project, 2011.

the relationship between time of day and people's behavior by looking at retweet activity from Twitter to see how the element of time of day impacted retweeting. He looked at a database of over 40 million retweets. As you can see from Figure 3.1, the amount of retweet activity that takes place between 4 pm and 6 pm is six times higher than the retweet activity that takes place between 8 am and 10 am.

All things being equal with respect to the information contained in the tweets and other variables, time of day can affect the use of a Communication Object. It impacts how people use the object, in this case the tweet. Applying this finding to a Project Environment, let's consider the project manager we mentioned above who sends out his report at 3 am. This finding suggests that the receiver's use of the report, and behavior in relation to the report, is affected by the element of time of day.

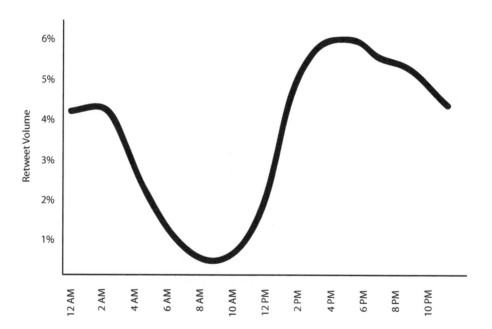

Figure 3.1   Retweet Activity by Hour

Source: Reproduced from *Zarrella's Hierarchy of Contagiousness*, The Domino Project, August 2013 with the kind permission of Seth Godin.

This finding on time of day is part of a larger study that Zarella carried out to see what factors affect the use of specific Communication Objects. Use is defined on a per study basis and is a reflection of the technology platform that generates the Communication Object being studied. For example, for one study of objects generated by e-mail, use is defined as opening the e-mail. For another study of objects generated by e-mail, use is defined as clicking on a link in the e-mail. For a study of objects generated by Twitter, use is defined as retweeting.

The studies look at elements besides the content of the Communication Object. They propose that, all things being equal, the difference in use of the object can be attributed to another element of the Communication Object aside from the content. These results show that other elements, besides the content in a Communication Object, affect the use of the object. You can get the content right, but if the other elements aren't aligned, the Communication Object won't achieve its goal—it won't be used in the intended way.

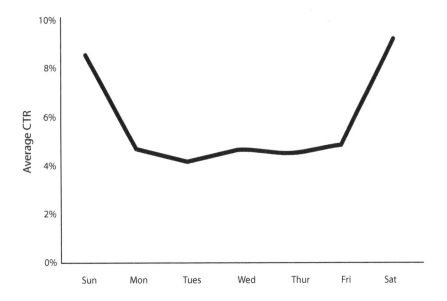

Figure 3.2   Day of the Week Impact on E-mail Click-throughs

Source: Reproduced from *Zarrella's Hierarchy of Contagiousness*, The Domino Project, August 2013 with the kind permission of Seth Godin.

Day of the Week

Here is another study by Zarella that looks at the impact of the day of the week (Figure 3.2). He studied a database of nearly 10 billion e-mail sends to see how the day of the week affected the click-through rate of an e-mail. The click-through rate (CTR) represents the number of people who click on a link in an e-mail which they receive. It is expressed in terms of a percentage of total e-mails sent. A CTR of 2 percent means that 2 percent of the people who received the e-mail clicked on a link in the e-mail. As you can see from Figure 3.2, the CTR on the weekend is nearly double the rate of a weekday.

All things being equal with respect to the information contained in the e-mail and other variables, the day of the week can affect the use of a Communication Object. Revisiting the communication strategy discussed in the example above where task information is sent out to the team via e-mail, this finding suggests that the day of the week on which that information is sent out will impact the use of that e-mail and therefore the use of the information contained in it.

How Much You Broadcast to an Audience

Zarella looked at the connection between a Twitter account's total output of links and the use of those links, defined as CTR on the link. As the graph in Figure 3.3 shows, the more links an account posted per hour, the lower the CTR on their links. The same result was found when the unit of time was changed to days.

All things being equal, the amount of communication we output to a particular audience over a period of time affects their use of that Communication Object. In a project context, this suggests that we should moderate and think about the amount of communication put out to a particular audience over any given period of time. For example, if we are constantly sending out e-mail updates, the likelihood of people reading each one decreases with the total number sent out.

Another implication of this result is that we should align the technology used to communicate with the intended use of the specific Communication Object output. Some technologies, like chat, cater to frequent communication. As we can see from the above result, the more frequent the communication output over a specific period of time, the more the recipient will filter out each subsequent communication. Project environments that use chat for distributing important information will have different outcomes from those that use infrequent meetings. When deciding on which technology tool to use for a particular type of communication, consider the expected frequency of communication output which that tool caters to and align the communication goals with the tools used.

A further result from the above observation is that once an account reached a certain output of links (around three links), the marginal difference in CTR from each additional link is close to zero. There is a saturation point for a given audience after which they stop paying attention. Once recipients decide to filter out information for that period of time on that media, it becomes impossible to get their attention.

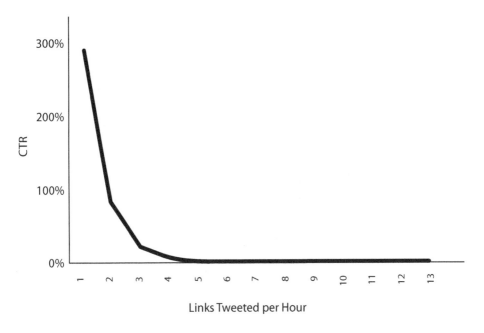

Figure 3.3   Click-through Rate by Links Tweeted per Hour
Source: Reproduced from *Zarrella's Hierarchy of Contagiousness*, The Domino Project, August 2013 with the kind permission of Seth Godin.

Readability, Word Choice and Emotional Tone

Zarella studied the readability of news stories posted on Facebook to see if there was any connection between this and how often it was shared. Readability was defined as the reading grade level of the text as measured by the Flesch-Kinkaid test which is built into Microsoft Word. There is a relationship between readability and sharing. The general trend is that the lower the reading grade level of the story, the more often it is shared.

In his study of articles posted on Facebook, Zarella observed that sharing varied according to the parts of speech in the titles of the articles. Titles that contained many adjectives or that were overly fancy were shared less often than those that were more simply made up of nouns and verbs. This suggests that word choice matters in how people use Communication Objects.

Zarella also studied his database of over 100 million retweets to find what words were contained in the most retweeted tweets and the least retweeted tweets. He saw that there were words that consistently showed up in the most retweeted tweets and different words that showed up in the least retweeted tweets. The specific words used affect the use of the Communication Objects produced. Some words are more conducive than others for achieving particular purposes. In other words, in the Project Environment, there are words that can be used that will help achieve the intended goal for the project and others that will make it harder to achieve the intended goal.

Zarella observed the relationship between the emotional tone of tweets and the number of followers on an account. The emotional tone was studied using two linguistic analysis programs, RID and LIWC. These programs analyze texts to determine the degree of positive or negative tone in the text. Zarella observed a direct correlation between negativity and the number of followers on an account. The more negative an account generally was, the fewer the number of people who wanted to listen to what that account was broadcasting. Followers vote with their feet—if they like to hear what someone is saying, they will follow that person; if they don't, they will unfollow that person and simply choose not to receive what is being tweeted. All things being equal with respect to the information contained in the Communication Object and other variables, readability, word choice and emotional tone affect the use of a Communication Object.

SPOTLIGHT: WORDS ARE FUZZY THINGS

At seminars I conduct, I commonly ask the seminar participants to write down five words that come to mind when they think about the word "food." Food is a part of everyone's life and is essential for our survival. There is no ambiguity on what is meant by the word "food." Yet, startlingly enough, as I go around and ask people for their five words, there is little commonality among the lists people come up with. No two people write down the same five words. At most, there is 75 percent commonality for one or two terms (generally "calories" and "healthy"). Occasionally, that is followed by a term with 30 percent commonality (often "socialization" or a related term) and most often only 2–15 percent of the people have any term in common (with terms like "cost", "clean-up," "family," "anticipation" and "wine"). Everyone knows what I'm talking about when I say "food," yet there is little commonality in what it means to each person.

The results are surprisingly similar when talking about seemingly common time-related terms.[i] Instead of writing down terms associated with the word "food," I say specific probability-related terms (such as "always," "never," "sometimes" and "often") and ask them to write down what percentage of the time something occurs if its occurrence can be described as happening "always." For example, if something always happens, what percentage of the time does that thing happen? I am always shocked at the range of probabilities people put and, again, how little commonality there is in the range. For the term "always," for example, results range from 50 percent of the time to 100 percent of the time, with limited commonality among participants. This means that everybody has their own, subjective sense of probability. Further, even when there is some commonality among participants in one term, e.g. "always" means 90 percent for two people, this doesn't automatically translate into those two people having the same probability for the other terms, e.g. "never" might mean 0 percent of the time for one of them and 10 percent of the time for the other. The same results are obtained when I run the experiment with time-related terms like "today," "tomorrow," "ASAP," "soon" and "end of day." Some people think "today" means "by close of business," while to others it means "before the business day starts tomorrow" or "before the 1 pm meeting tomorrow where you'll need the information."

---

i   This exercise comes from the paper "An Experiential Classroom Exercise to Improve Communication Effectiveness" by Terence L. Holmes and Edward C. Brewer from Murray State University in Murray, KY, May 2006, listed under the Archive of Marketing Education. The results discussed in the paper concur with the results I experience in my seminars.

Audience Characteristics

The relationship between items like readability or word choice and sharing, or emotional tone and followers, is not strictly linear and likely reflects characteristics of the audience who receive the Communication Object. For example, people who post stories written at a ninth-grade reading level may have more friends that appreciate stories written at a ninth-grade reading level than people who post stories that have a seventh-grade reading level. The people who see the seventh-grade level posts may be looking for stories at a higher or lower reading level. We can't create simple rules that apply to all situations. Each audience has their own characteristics. In our Project Environment, different audiences will react differently to the Communication Objects we broadcast.

It seems obvious to state that the use of Communication Objects will vary depending on how aligned it is with the characteristics of the intended audience. However, managers often expect everyone in a Project Environment to react in the same way when presented with the same information. This is not the case. Different audiences will react differently to the same piece of information, depending on the characteristics of the audience. Take, for example, a detailed project schedule down to five levels of subtasks that is sent out to everyone in a Project Environment. A group of project sponsors interested in overall project progress who receive that schedule will react differently to it compared to the team leaders whose team members are the people doing the work on those tasks.

Total Quantity of Information a Person Receives

It is estimated that we receive two million bits of information per second through our five senses, yet we are only capable of processing around seven chunks of information at any point in time.[3] Our brains automatically sift through information and decide what we pay attention to. Adding more information to an environment doesn't increase our capacity to process the information—it adds to the amount of filtering we have to do.

---

3 Mihaly Csikszentmihalyi, *Flow: The Psychology of Optimal Experience*. New York: HarperCollins, 2008. There is some debate as to whether seven is the "magic" number for human data processing. Whether the number is seven or not is less relevant than the filtering that occurs.

The total volume of information we receive is a factor that determines what we do with the information we receive. The greater the volume, the more the sender has to rely on the receiver to decide to let the information come through the filter. Not all information makes it through the filter. And if it does, the act of filtering reduces the chances that any single specific piece of information will be acted upon. The total volume of information also affects the amount of potential attention that any one piece of information receives— the higher the volume, the less attention available. This affects what will be done with the information. Moreover, the quantity of information is related to how dependant the sender is on the receiver's prioritization of information. The higher the quantity of information, the more the receiver has to decide what to prioritize even among the pieces of information that have made it through the filter.

In a Project Environment, this means that the more information someone receives about the project, the more filtering they have to do. The more information there is about the project impacts how any single piece of project information is utilized by the receiver. For example, team members who have to participate in meetings where updates are given on every single task on the project have to do much more filtering of project information than team members who only receive information on tasks that are directly relevant to them. For example, project participants who are cc'd into every e-mail about the project have to do much more filtering than participants who only receive e-mails that are relevant to them.

From a manager's perspective, the quantity of information they receive impacts what they do with that information. For example, managers who receive a high volume of change requests from stakeholders have to do a lot more filtering than managers which receive a lower volume of requests. This impacts the total throughput of requests which will be dealt with, the time it takes to deal with requests and the attention that will be paid to each request over a given period of time. For example, take a manager who receives a copy of every iteration of a document as it is being produced—that manager has to do a lot more filtering than a manager who only receives the final copy for their review. This impacts the manager's engagement with the document, the attention paid to the document and the total number of documents they can have in process at any point in time.

SPOTLIGHT: CUT THROUGH CLUTTER LIKE A VIRAL VIDEO

Given the amount of information people receive on a daily basis, it can be a daunting and time-consuming task to design a Communication Object that will reach your intended audience. Not every Communication Object needs the same amount of work, but for those that need to make a big impact, the work put into it is worthwhile. Here is a short case study of some students in Montreal, Canada who invested an incredible amount of work into a Communication Object and reaped the rewards.

In mid-2012, students at a Montreal design school were asked "How do you make a video that gets 100,000 views on the Internet?" This was their project. They would get an "A" if they got 100,000 views. They researched common themes behind viral videos, brainstormed story ideas and put in over 500 hours creating a video. The result was a one-minute video that garnered over two million views in its first 24 hours and more than 36 million views in its first week.[i] That is remarkable (they got the "A") and it is a great case study on designing Communication Objects to attain a specific outcome. YouTube is a tangible example of information overload; 72 hours of video are uploaded to YouTube every minute.[ii] This means that you could watch videos for more than 11 years and still not be done with just one day's worth of video uploaded to YouTube.

Among all that competition, most videos receive fewer than 100 views[iii] within their first month. This one-minute-worth of video in our case study received two million views in a day out of a total of 6.2 million minutes of video uploaded in just that one day.

The videographers designed an effective Communication Object that cut through a massive amount of clutter. They made it through the volume of competing information and through each viewer's filter of attention. Their project attained and widely surpassed the project's goal of getting 100,000 views. They did so by paying attention to the Communication Object they were creating, understanding the environment in which the Communication Object will live and investing time into the Communication Object. They researched, planned and spent a huge amount of time executing a one-minute video. It is estimated that the team spent over 500 hours on that video.[iv] How many managers spend that amount of time on communication? As we can see from the video, the investment paid off. The 500 hours they put into the one-minute video generated over 600,000 hours of viewing in one week. It reached tens of millions of people, garnered an inestimable amount of attention around the world and airtime with major news networks.

i   "Golden Eagle Snatches Kid," http://www.youtube.com/watch?feature=player_embedded&v=CE0Q904gtMI.
ii   http://www.youtube.com/t/press_statistics.
iii Estimate, extrapolating from http://www.reelseo.com/average-number-youtube-views-month.
iv   NBC report on The Today Show, http://www.hulu.com/watch/437204, 20 December 2012.

It takes a lot to cut through the clutter: an understanding of the environment, the medium and the audience. Each set of circumstances is unique, requiring dedicating time and effort to understand the unique Project Environment and the audiences.

The videographers started by having an explicit goal around which to design their Communication Object. They wanted to create a viral video that people would share. With that in mind, they began the process of determining the content for the video.[v] They researched their audience's favorite topics. What topics, what content would cross boundaries and reach as wide an audience as possible? They discovered that it was animals and babies. If you've ever spent time on YouTube or watching television shows like *America's Funniest Home Videos*, this may not come as a surprise.[vi] The topic, the content of the video, directly contributes to it being believable and thus making it through the boundary.[vii]

Once the videographers picked the general topic, they brainstormed on a storyline. It had to make an impact but be believable enough that people would watch it. In addition, part of their assignment was to integrate computer generated imagery (CGI) with real footage. The storyline had to lend itself to the parameters of the assignment and be able to be filmed in a way that added to the believability. For example, the way the video was shot, with a pan across the sky following an eagle and then a seemingly unintentional view of the grass as the videographer runs to check on the baby, all created context that made the video look real.

With the topic and storyline decided, the team set to work on creating the geometry of the CGI baby and CGI eagle in 3D, rigging the geometries with a bone system so they would "move" realistically, then shape and edit them into the real footage. The video was made with off-the-shelf equipment and software. It didn't require Hollywood-level special effects; in fact, it may not have been as widely viewed had it looked too perfect. The medium, the style, the narrative and the feel all contributed to it crossing into people's boundaries, making it past their filters, being believed and passed on. Some people found it through their online network. Some, like myself, heard about it around a dinner table. Others saw it on broadcast television or in an online news source. Being encased and delivered by seemingly credible sources contributed to its proliferation.

---

v   CNN interview with the creators of the video, http://www.cnn.com/video/?%20%20hpt=hp_c2#/video/bestoftv/2012/12/20/exp-point-eagle-hoax.cnn, 20 December 2012.

vi   I will point out that they described the topics in a broad enough way as to allow for the animal to be an eagle. Had they gone with a tighter definition, they would have tried to do something with cats.

vii The host of NBC's *The Today Show* (20 December 2012) said "Of course I believed it. It had a baby in it." http://www.hulu.com/watch/437204.

Interestingly, as the video started to spread, it reached a point where people spent time dissecting it frame by frame to spot clues as to its veracity. The final product wasn't perfect; there were inconsistencies that led some people to conclude that it was a fake.[viii] However, this didn't stop it from spreading. The target environment in which it was spreading didn't much care. By the time people were discussing whether it was real or not, the sheer quantity of views and the nature of its transmission (e.g. people were sharing the video on Facebook with their circle of friends and it was being e-mailed and tweeted around) meant that interest in the video grew. The Communication Object was an unquestionable success. Not every Communication Object needs this level of effort, but for those that do, investing the time makes a big difference in terms of the results.

---

viii At one point in its initial flight, the eagle's wing is missing. As it approaches the ground, its shadow appears, disappears and reappears. The creators took pride in the fact that people were willing to engage enough with the video to spend time going through it frame by frame.

Boundaries between Groups

People in different groups have their own set of filters on information and their own way of expressing information. These filters and ways of expressing information form a boundary around the group. The existence of boundaries is a feature of the Communication Environment that directly impacts how Communication Objects are used and the solution delivered by that Project Environment. Project environments that facilitate communication across boundaries produce different solutions from those that don't.

The boundaries define how a member of the group interprets and reacts to a given Communication Object. The boundaries also define how a member of the group will express a given piece of information. In other words, it will define elements of the Communication Object which a member of the group will create. One example of a boundary is the specialized language and training of a profession. Engineers speak a very different language compared to medical doctors. Both are highly trained professional specialties, but they have different languages, as it were. If the two groups are supposed to work together on a medical device, they need to find a common terminology. Geography and culture can create another set of boundaries between groups in a Project Environment. This can be felt in ways as simple as what system of measurement people use. As we saw with the Mars Orbiter, that difference alone was sufficient to cause project failure.

SPOTLIGHT: BOUNDARIES WITHIN US MILITARY DECISION MAKING

General Stanley McChrystal discussed the phenomena of boundaries within the US military decision-making process in an interview on *The Daily Show with Jon Stewart*.[i] McChrystal is a retired four-star general who led the war in Afghanistan from June 2009 to June 2010. He retired for what many consider to be political reasons.

Jon Stewart, the interviewer, asked him if civilian politics got in the way of military decision making. McChrystal responded by pointing out that civilians and military personnel come from different backgrounds and each have their own language. This difference is accentuated in an all-volunteer, professional military such as that in the US where most of the leadership are lifelong military professionals. The civilian and military don't often interact with each other as they are each coming up the ranks of their respective career tracks. So, when the civilian and military leadership have to get together to make decisions, it can take a big effort and a lot of time. "Everyone is trying to do the right thing," he said. "I didn't see anyone who wasn't trying to get a good outcome." But the cultural and linguistic challenges can make it a challenging and time-consuming process for everyone to work together. The boundaries get in the way.

He mentioned that it took President Abraham Lincoln two to two-and-a-half years to figure out how to interact with senior military, and for senior military to learn how to work with him. People have to learn how to understand each other, particularly when they speak different languages and see things differently from each other. Once President Lincoln and the senior military leadership figured out how to interact with each other, the tide of the Civil War turned in Lincoln's favor.

---

i   *The Daily Show with Jon Stewart*, interview with Stanley McChrystal, extended interview part 3, 8 January 2013, http://www.thedailyshow.com/watch/tue-january-8-2013/exclusive---stanley-mcchrystal-extended-interview-pt--3.

Is it a Boundary Object?

Communication Objects that are meant for a wide and diverse audience need to be able to speak to each group in that audience. For example, a mission statement for a project needs to speak to everyone in the Project Environment. A Communication Object that can meaningfully cross boundaries is called a boundary object. A boundary object[4] is an artifact whose meaning, while

---

4   The term "boundary object" was coined by the sociologist Susan Leigh Star in 1988.

different for different groups, has sufficient commonality across each group that everyone knows what everyone is talking about. For example, when I talk about a dog, I mean a house pet. When a veterinarian talks about a dog, they mean a patient. When someone who shows dogs talks about a dog, they mean a potential contestant in a dog show. Each of us uses the term according to our context and within our boundaries. Nonetheless, we all know what we're talking about when we use the word "dog." Project environments that utilize boundary objects produce different solutions from those that don't.

The Process that Generates the Communication Object

The process which generates a Communication Object affects a Project Environment's Solution Delivery Capabilities. For example, a Project Environment that uses a risk register generated through individual interviews will produce different solutions from a Project Environment that uses a risk register generated through group workshops. The content of the risk registers may or may not be different, but, significantly, the relationships between the people in the Project Environment will be different and their approach to risks, as the risks materialize, will be different. Consequently, the solution delivered by those environments will be different.

This was demonstrated by Dr David Hancock in his analysis of the risk registers produced by two different processes on the same project,[5] the development of Heathrow Airport's Terminal 5. The first process, conducted in 1996, was in line with traditional risk management approaches, while the second, conducted in 2000, departed from traditional processes. Differences included the scope of the process, the type of people who participated, the role of the facilitator and how participants interacted. Both processes generated risk registers, albeit that the nature of the risks recorded differed. However, the most significant effect of the different processes was in the type of relationships established among the participants through the process of generating the risk register. The type of relationships established by the first process were the same ones seen in numerous development projects and which, the author contends, do little to prevent catastrophic failures on development projects.[6] In contrast, the type of relationships established by the second process

5   David Hancock and Robin Holt, "Tame, Messy and Wicked Problems in Risk Management," Manchester Metropolitan University Business School Working Paper Series (Online) WPS054, September 2003.
6   The author cites the 1994 collapse of a subway tunnel, the Heathrow Express, which was called "the worst civil engineering disaster in the UK in the last quarter century."

built a Communication Environment which facilitated the recognition and resolution of complex, interconnected risk drivers. This different approach to the risk management process resulted[7] in the delivery of a safe development, Terminal 5, which was delivered on time and on budget.

What it Means for Us

Communication Object elements are non-content-specific descriptors of Communication Objects. They tell us about the Communication Object and are the result of applying analytic tools to the objects in a Communication Environment. Since the objects in an environment, and how they are used, are defined by the design of the Communication Environment, studying Communication Object elements allows us to better understand the Communication Environment.

Further, we saw that people's behavior is affected by the elements of a Communication Object. For example, the more e-mails people receive, the less likely they are to pay attention to any one specific e-mail. Therefore, we can use the analysis of Communication Object elements to isolate and identify which elements are related to specific behaviors of people in our Project Environment and to specific behaviors of the Project Environment as a whole. Once identified, we can manage the Communication Object elements to improve the chances that a particular person in the Project Environment, or the Project Environment itself, will deliver the desired outcomes.

We have discussed only a few Communication Object elements to make the point that there is a connection between Communication Object elements and people's behavior. There are many other elements to a Communication Object. Different Communication Object elements can be generated by applying an analytic tool or technique to a Communication Object. The list of potential elements that can be isolated and managed is constrained only by the range of analytic tools and techniques applied to the observation of Communication Objects. It is up to us to determine the elements worth generating, isolating and analyzing for our specific environments. Other elements could include the following:

---

7   "The most important difference between Terminal 5 and other large building projects has been the approach to project management, and especially to risk." From "Terminal 5—Blue Skies Thinking. Heathrow's New Terminal is on Time and on Budget. How Odd," *The Economist*, 18 August 2005, http://www.economist.com/node/4300209.

- The phase of the project in which the Communication Object is broadcast, similar to the time of day.

- The number of tasks on a person's plate, similar to total volume of information a person receives but often an easier number to track, or how many total projects a person is managing.

- The level of trust in the sender, which is gauged using tools and techniques from psychology and sociology such as validated self-report questionnaires.

- The centrality of the sender in a network diagram of the Project Environment, using techniques from the field of network analysis.

To conclude this chapter, a Communication Object is a multi-faceted data point that unlocks information about the Communication Environment and the Project Environment's Solution Delivery Capabilities. Communication Object elements help us to understand the Communication Environment, the people in it and how a Communication Object will be used. Expanding the types of questions we ask about the Communication Object helps us to probe the environment's solution delivery capabilities to uncover the factors that affect project outcomes. Understanding these factors allows us to tailor the elements to improve a Project Environment's solution delivery capabilities.

4

Observable Behaviors of a Project Environment

Project environments have observable behaviors, just as recipients of Communication Objects do. These are the aggregate outcomes of people in the Project Environment. For example, schedule variance (SV) is an observable behavior of a Project Environment. It tells us how far ahead or behind schedule the project is running and is a function of people's behavior in the Project Environment.

There are many other observable behaviors of a Project Environment. For example, we can look at the revenue generated by a Project Environment, its overall profitability or its profit margin. We can gage the Project Environment's ability to create innovative products or its ability to produce low-cost products. We can look at an environment's adoption rate of a new software tool, new project management methodology or new idea. We can measure the average number of years of employment of people in a Project Environment, the turnover rate or the promotion rate from within the environment. We can measure the level of trust within an environment. We can observe the network diagram of people within the Project Environment. These are a few examples of other observable behaviors of a Project Environment.

The observable behaviors are generated through the application of analytic tools and techniques to a Project Environment. The tools' output tells us about the Project Environment and gives us variables we can use to design, plan, control and manage our Project Environments. Accounting tools and techniques tell us about revenue and profitability. Market analysis tells us about innovation and relative costs. Survey research tells us about adoption rates. Human Resources Department tools tell us about the employment characteristics of the people in the environment. Psychological and sociological analytic tools tell us about trust and group dynamics of a

Project Environment. Network analysis tells us about the relationships between people and groups in a Project Environment. We can apply a myriad of analytic tools and techniques to generate observable behaviors of a Project Environment.

Metrics from the earned value management approach to measuring and managing project performance provide further observable behaviors of a Project Environment. These include SV, cost variance (CV), the schedule performance index (SPI) and the cost performance index (CPI). The variances tell us how far ahead or behind the Project Environment is compared to our anticipated value for either schedule (SV) or cost (CV). The indices tell us at what rate the Project Environment moved ahead or behind the anticipated value for either schedule (SPI) or cost (CPI).

We can observe, measure and track the observable behaviors of a Project Environment. We can then compare the behaviors against Communication Design elements of the Project Environment and elements of the Communication Objects used in the Project Environment. The observable behaviors of a Project Environment, like those of an individual recipient, reflect the design elements of the Communication Environment, the elements of the Communication Objects in the environment and the decision-making processes of people in the Project Environment. Therefore, by comparing the design and object elements with the Project Environment's observable behaviors, we can better understand the relationship between these elements and the Project Environment's observable behaviors. This improves our understanding of the factors that contribute to a Project Environment's observable behaviors and, as such, it improves our understanding of the elements we can plan for, design with, manage and control in order to change a Project Environment's behavior.

Examples of the Relationship between a Communication Object and the Observable Behavior of a Project Environment

VOLUME OF E-MAILS AND SCHEDULE PERFORMANCE

Let's say we have a hypothetical Project Environment that consistently misses deadlines. It always delivers late. We want to improve its schedule performance so that it can deliver on time. We can use the observable behavior of SV to track schedule performance and the SPI to track the rate at which we are attaining schedule performance. We can use the observable elements of communication design and Communication Objects to understand and improve schedule performance.

For our hypothetical Project Environment, let's consider the number of e-mails allowed to be sent in any given week. Let's assume that there are no restrictions on the number of e-mails sent or any restrictions on who can talk to whom in the Project Environment. We consistently observe that once we are 20 percent into the schedule on any project, the SV is negative, we are behind schedule and that the SPI is steady at 0.75, so we are attaining schedule at a rate that is 75 percent of what we thought we would. We also observe that we are generating e-mails at a rate of 100 e-mails per week, given the current number of people in the Project Environment. We observe this using the existing reporting capabilities of e-mail software programs such as Microsoft Exchange.

We decide to implement a more defined communication strategy to improve schedule performance. We restrict the number of e-mails sent in the environment to 50 per week and we then track SPI after the new communication strategy has been in place for a meaningful period of time. We observe that the SPI is now 0.85 and rising. We have improved the Project Environment's ability to attain schedule. Impressed with the results, we go a step further in more tightly defining a communication strategy. We implement content guidelines and specify that all e-mails have to be 200 words or less. We then track the SPI after a meaningful period of time and see that it has risen to 1.00, so we are now attaining schedule at a rate consistent with our initial estimate of schedule performance. We also observe that people are spending more time on the phone communicating with team members rather than using e-mail.

Before we go any further, a critical clarification is necessary. Schedule performance is not driven by the observable elements of Communication Design or communication elements. Neither the number of e-mails sent in a Project Environment, nor the content of those e-mails, drives schedule performance. Schedule performance is driven by people's behavior; it is driven by people working towards delivery. People's behavior, though, is shaped by the number of e-mails they receive and the content of those e-mails. By managing the observable design and object elements of the Communication Environment, such as the number of e-mails and their content, we can shape and manage people's behavior. In doing so, we can improve schedule performance.

Here is another hypothetical, this time related to attaining technical performance. Let's assume we have a Project Environment that consistently fails to deliver what the customer needs. We observe that all participants in the Project Environment use a requirements document to define what the customer needs. The customer helps put it together, signs off on it and the project delivery team works exactly to the requirements document. The solution delivered meets the requirements document exactly, but the solutions delivered are consistently not what the customer needs.

We decide to change the format of the Communication Object used to define what the customer needs. Instead of using a requirements document, the project delivery team builds prototypes and delivers them to the customer. The customer evaluates the prototypes and provides feedback to the project delivery team. The team integrates this feedback into a future prototype and delivers it to the customer. This iterative cycle continues until the project delivery team delivers the final product to the customer. After a meaningful period of time of using the new format for defining customers' needs, we observe an improvement in the Project Environment's capability to deliver exactly what the customer wants. We also observe an increase in communication between the customer and the project delivery team.

There may be numerous explanations as to why a change in the elements of communication design or objects alters a Project Environment's Solution Delivery Capabilities. In the first hypothetical, people may have spent too much time focusing on filtering information and responding to e-mails instead of spending time on getting work done. Thus, by limiting the number of e-mails, we reduced the amount of information they had to filter through and sharpened the focus on getting work done. In the second hypothetical, there may have been uncertainty around the words used in the requirements document. The customer may not have known how to put into words exactly what they want or they may not have known exactly what they want. Alternatively, the customer and project deliver team may have used the same words but understood them differently. By creating prototypes, we reduced the uncertainty. The customer and project delivery team had a tangible boundary object that they could discuss. This reduced uncertainty on the requirements. On the other hand, the reason could be completely something else. There can be multiple and diverse reasons, but we can still use changes in a Communication Environment to manage and improve a Project Environment's Solution Delivery Capabilities.

Changing elements of the Communication Objects changes the environment's Solution Delivery Capabilities, as evidenced by observable behaviors of the Project Environment.

MISSION STATEMENT TO ENHANCE THE USE OF EVM IN US DEPARTMENT OF DEFENSE

There is a US government office mandated to improve the clarity of information on over a trillion dollars' worth of project. The proposed method to fulfill the mandate is to enhance the way EVM is used across projects. Specifically, the proposed method is for all participants to use EVM as the de facto language of project performance tracking. Leadership wants to replicate the successful environment of the F/A-18 E/F across all projects.

The man charged with implementing this method began his initiative by putting out a mission statement and presenting it to the engineers and scientists who worked on those projects. The observable behavior he was looking for was an increase in the adoption of EVM on projects. This didn't happen. He then developed and implemented ways to make the engineers and scientists understand the importance of his mission statement. He then tried to explain to them how his mission statement was beneficial to them. Nothing happened. He developed training material to teach them how important it was for them to adopt EVM. In parallel, he investigated using or developing regulations, with punitive consequences for failure to comply, that would force the engineers and scientists to see things his way. They resisted adoption. When we met, he was exasperated and felt he was now locked into a battle of personalities and power. He was intelligently executing a worthwhile goal and was not seeing as much progress as he would have liked to.

After hearing the story, I asked to see the initial mission statement. It had the right content and the information it contained was accurate, but it was the wrong mission statement for what he wanted to accomplish. The words and the tone used to convey the information were wrong for the intended audience and desired actions. He wanted to observe an increase in adoption from a diverse group of people and he wanted them to be interested in learning about EVM. He hadn't achieved this. So, rather than revisit the mission statement, the message he was conveying, he looked for ways to say it louder and more forcefully, which didn't work.

I suggested he revisit the mission statement. That conclusion came from focusing on the Communication Environment and its relation to the mission he was executing. He had a goal of seeing an observable change in the Project Environment, namely, an increase in adoption of EVM. He created a Communication Object to help him attain the goal. It didn't help him. Therefore, we needed to look at the Communication Object in more detail and analyze the observable elements of the object. The contents of the Communication Object were accurate, but that was not sufficient to change the behavior of the Project Environment. Other elements of the Communication Object needed to be changed in order to change people's behavior. We began looking at creating boundary objects. This seems to be bearing fruit for attaining the desired change in the Project Environment.

People will not suddenly see the new mission statement and start to behave differently, but the mission statement, as a Communication Object, has ripple effects on people's behavior. Getting the object right goes a long way toward changing behavior. Billions of dollars are spent every year on advertising agencies to do just that. Consumer goods companies want advertising agencies to come up with the right object to influence people's behavior. It takes more than accurate wording; it takes the right Communication Object.

MISSION STATEMENT FOR HEATHROW TERMINAL 5

The mission statement for the Heathrow Terminal 5 project changed between the 1996 risk workshop and the 2000 risk workshop. The change in the mission statement contributed to the changed outcome of the risk workshops and the successful delivery of the Terminal.

The project's mission statement in 1996 was "the delivery of a terminal commensurate with its role as an international gateway to the United Kingdom, set within the BAA Board's approved rates of return, and with the minimal possible environmental impact."[1] In order to deliver the Terminal within the range of specific parameters, the project was broken down into subprojects focused on specific parameters, namely, "technical and financial issues using quantified measures covering cost, program, environment,

---

1   Hancock and Holt, "Tame, Messy and Wicked Problems in Risk Management." While there
     may have been a more elegant mission statement, Hancock and Holt's description portrays a
     multi-parameter, muddled view of the desired end-state with potential inherent conflicts. For
     clarification, BAA owns Heathrow Airport and others. It was formed from the British Airports
     Authority in 1986.

quality and safety."[2] Engineers and accountants were brought in to identify potential risks and plan risk responses. The risk workshop facilitator ensured that participants' expertise and problem-solving abilities were thoroughly utilized. The resultant risk register produced by the process focused primarily on technical and financial risks and ways to fix them. This was in line with a traditional approach to risk management. The probability distribution of the Project Environment delivering a project that was safe, on time and on budget could be expected to be no different from those of other projects using this approach.

The mission statement in 2000 changed. It became "To develop the world's most refreshing interchange delivered within cost and program parameters, maximizing shareholder value and respecting last responsible moment to realize exceptional project performance."[3] According to Hancock and Holt, this change in the mission statement made a huge difference to the risk workshop and the overall approach to risk management on the project. First, it changed the type of people that needed to be included in the risk workshop. Second, it changed the types of problems and solutions that would be identified in the workshop, directly impacting the contents of the risk register. Finally, it changed how the participants would work together, the language and techniques they would use, and the relationships they would form through participation in the risk workshop.

To quote the paper:

> The inclusion of last responsible moment meant the framing of the risk workshop changed from an emphasis upon delivering problem-solution coefficients to articulating those practices that afforded the project team the greatest space for reflection upon the nature of the problems they faced, before having to take a decision. This emphasis upon reflection and conversation meant it was considered critical to choose the participants based on their influence and ability to explore prevailing and emerging business issues.[4]

The design and execution of the second risk workshop changed because of the new mission statement. The facilitator set up an environment centered on uncovering underlying assumptions and perceptions of a risk rather than

---

2   Ibid.
3   Ibid., pp. 14–15.
4   Ibid., p. 15.

the technical identification and accuracy of that risk. To avoid any sense of judgment, the risk register color-coded potential risks rather than listing them by number. As such, there was no number one biggest risk; there were only risks that were big risks to the project (coded red), medium risks (coded yellow) and low risks (coded green). The resultant risk register primarily focused on risks stemming from the social interaction of various groups on the project. This new approach fundamentally changed the Project Environment. To quote the authors:

> Terminal 5 underwent an entire identity shift, from a technically constructed asset owned by a single company to a transport interchange invested in by many stakeholders.

> The process aimed to replace the identification of reactive, fire-fighting activities with pro-active approaches by improving project team confidence, knowledge awareness and clear activity responsibility communicated through the life of the project.

> ... active consideration was given to the risks associated with project team "skills" integration, stakeholder involvement and communication channels as well to the "technical" risks.[5]

The new approach changed the probability distribution of the Project Environment delivering a successful project. And, as *The Economist* pointed out, this approach drove the improved performance of the Project Environment and was a significant factor in the Terminal being safely delivered on time and on budget. The new approach was predicated by a change in the mission statement. From this, we can see how a change in a Communication Object, the mission statement, can ripple through the Project Environment and change the project delivery capabilities of that environment.

FORMAT OF A PROBLEM AND HELPING SLOW THE SPREAD OF HIV

In September 2011, the media[6] announced that a group of computer gamers had solved a piece of the AIDS puzzle that had evaded professional scientists for 15 years. The gamers solved it in 10 days. This was accomplished

---

5   Ibid.
6   "Gamers Decode AIDS Protein that Stumped Researchers for 15 Years in Just 3 Weeks,"
     Huffington Post, 19 September 2011, http://www.huffingtonpost.com/2011/09/19/aids-protein-
     decoded-gamers_n_970113.html.

through a website called Fold.it,[7] which publishes a computer gaming program for working on geometric puzzles, like origami meets Tetris. Fold.it focuses specifically on the area of decoding complex proteins in the field of bio-chemistry. Anyone can download and use the program. Scientists than formulate an existing scientific problem for the gaming program and let the gaming community go at it. The better the model that a team produces, the more points a team gets. This particular challenge, modeling the Mason-Pfizer monkey virus (M-PMV) retroviral protease, could help scientists to develop a drug that slows the spread of the HIV virus. Scientists had been working on it for 15 years. By changing the Communication Object, the problem was solved in 10 days, with no cost for the gamers' labor.

SPOTLIGHT: CHANGING THE INSTITUTIONAL CONTEXT TO LAUNCH THE COMMERCIAL SPACE SECTOR

One element of the Communication Environment is the institutional context surrounding the Project Environment. Changing the institutional context can change the environment's Solution Delivery Capabilities. Take, for example, the Ansari X-Prize. The X-Prize changes the context of a problem. Instead of making it a corporate goal or policy initiative, it creates grand challenges with cash awards for whoever can solve the problem. Teams compete for the prize. They can come from academia or industry and take completely novel approaches to solving the problem. The teams aren't encumbered by an institutional context that predefines solutions; the only thing that matters is solving the problem.

One of the most notable success stories was the Ansari X-Prize to "build and launch a spacecraft capable of carrying three people to 100 kilometers above the earth's surface, twice within two weeks."[i] It was won by a private team led by Burt Rutan, an aerospace designer, and Paul Allen, a financier and co-founder of Microsoft. It was the birth of the burgeoning private space industry. The Ansari X-Prize itself was modeled on the Orteig Prize, which was won by Charles Lindbergh in 1927 and helped launch the modern commercial airline industry. Changing the context of the Project Environment changes the type of solutions that the environment can produce.

---

i   See the X-Prize Foundation website http://space.xprize.org/ansari-x-prize.

---

7   http://fold.it/portal/info/about.

What it Means for Us

We can combine observations of multiple elements and the observable behaviors of a Project Environment to get a comprehensive view of the Communication Environment and its impact on an environment's Solution Delivery Capabilities. For example, I have seen programs where the solution delivered met the requirements documentation, but was not what the customer wanted. This has occurred even in programs where the customer was involved in the generation of the requirements documentation and signed off on them. Clearly, something went wrong. However, an analysis of the content of the requirements document alone did not yield answers as to why the program missed the mark because the solution exactly met the requirements. Instead, we had to look at other elements to understand what went wrong.

The combined view of Communication Object elements and design elements provides an analytic tool for Project Performance Management. We can use the analysis to understand the drivers of project performance in our Project Environments. We can manage and improve the Solution Delivery Capabilities of our Project Environments by understanding the drivers of project performance.

Here is a list of the elements of Communication Objects and design elements in the Communication Environment which we can look at to understand the drivers of project performance. These are also the variables that we can design with, plan with and manage to improve the performance of a Project Environment. This list only contains those variables which we have previously discussed; as mentioned above, there are others.

Elements of Communication Objects	Design Elements of the Communication Environment
➤ Time of Day	➤ Organizing Teams
➤ Day of the Week	➤ Locating Teams
➤ How Much You Broadcast to an Audience	➤ Assigning Tasks
➤ Readability	➤ Describing Task Information
➤ Emotional Tone	➤ Coordinating Activity
➤ Word Choice	➤ Who Can Talk to Who in a Project
➤ Audience Characteristics	Environment
➤ Total Quantity of Information a Person Receives	➤ Setting Rules for Each Method
	➤ Defining the Method for Specific Subject-Matter Domains
➤ Boundaries between Groups	
➤ Is it a Boundary Object?	➤ The Schedule of Communication
➤ The Process that Generates the Communication Object	➤ The Workflow of Communication
	➤ Communication Strategy

As we look at the list, it is easy to notice that there is overlap and interconnectedness among the variables. For example, "Day of the Week" is directly related to "The Schedule of Communication." This means that we can use isolated information on how the use of a Communication Object varies according to the day of the week to build our schedule of communication. To give another example, "Word Choice" is related to "Describing Task Information." Therefore, we can use isolated information on how the use of a Communication Object varies by "Word Choice" to create guidelines for how task information should be described. However, it can fast become complicated, as we can see when we note that "Word Choice" is impacted by "Audience Characteristics" and "Boundaries between Groups." Which audiences are relevant is determined by "Organizing Teams" and "Assigning Tasks," i.e. how teams are organized and how tasks are assigned. Then, depending on the way an environment is organized, "Is it a Boundary Object?" becomes a relevant variable. A Communication Environment is complex and multi-faceted. Considering that a Project Environment's Solution Delivery Capabilities are the result of many people working together, the fact that it is complex, multi-faceted and interconnected makes sense.

To conclude this chapter, Project Environments have observable behaviors. These include task delivery-specific items such as on-time and on-budget delivery. These can also include behaviors such as an environment's ability to innovate, create new knowledge or adopt a new process. An environment's behavior is a result of the aggregate outcomes of the decision making and action of the people in the environment. As such, a Project Environment's behavior is directly impacted by the Communication Environment, specifically the Communication Design decisions and the elements of Communication Objects. By using communication as a Performance Management Tool, we can better understand the relationship between specific elements of the Communication Environment and specific Project Environment behaviors. We can then use our understanding of this relationship to better design, plan, manage and control our Project Environments, enhancing the likelihood of the Project Environment exhibiting the desired observable behavior and delivering the desired outcomes.

5

Using Communication as a Performance Management Tool

We can formalize the technique of using communication as a Performance Management Tool. This formalization puts communication in the context of Performance Management Tools already in use, such as EVM.

The formal technique starts with producing a baseline of planned, or expected, communication. An environment that makes deliberate Communication Design decisions and enforces them can produce a baseline of expected communication. This baseline can then be used to measure how actual communication differs from expected communication within the Project Environment. This measurement can be combined with other performance management metrics, such as the SPI. This allows us to more finely map the relationship between changes in management efforts to improve project performance through communication and the changes in a specific performance management metric, such as SPI.

Environments that utilize formalized Project Performance Management systems such as EVM can create EVM-type communication metrics to measure the impact that changes in communication have on other performance management metrics. Like any EVM system, the quality of the data depends on how well controlled the baseline is. In the case of capturing the impact of performance management using communication, this translates into how deliberate the Communication Design decisions are and how strictly they are enforced. In an environment with deliberate design and strict enforcement, we can create and maintain a baseline of expected communication. We can then measure and manage communication as a Performance Management Tool using EVM-type metrics. Take the following example.

Let's assume a simplified environment with a well-defined communication strategy such as the one we described in Chapter 1. Additional steps have been added for the sake of this example. Let's say there is one project manager, one team leader and five team members. We can use the following table (Table 5.1) to create an estimate of the number of e-mails generated during a particular period of time on the project for a particular process. Specifically, for this simplified example, we are estimating the number of e-mails generated by the process of distributing task information to team members.

The estimate of the number of e-mails generated over a specific period of time is parallel to the step of time phasing a budget to develop a performance management baseline (PMB) in EVM. In fact, the time-phased estimate of the number of e-mails can be integrated into a PMB, as we will see in the table. We are estimating the number of e-mails because that is what our communication strategy defines and allows us to measure. If the communication strategy were defined in terms of other communication methods or if we chose to measure all communication methods in a strategy, we could.

This is not as onerous as it sounds and will become even easier over time. There are existing tools which can log and count e-mails, easily generating this kind of data. The same is true with many technology-based methods of communication. There are analytic tools which can be applied to communication to generate observable and measurable elements for many forms of electronic communication. Further, we are in the early stages of our use of electronic communications. It will become even easier to do this kind of analysis just as doing EVM became easier with the advent of better accounting tools and software. The tools and the toolset to measure it will develop over time.

In environments without a well-defined communication strategy we can create baselines of expected communication using other techniques. For example, we can use the number of communication channels in the environment, estimate how much each person speaks to each other per week using a specific communication method and come up with an estimate of communication. We can base the estimate on our past experience with the people involved or on observation. Alternatively, we can base it on a communication plan that spells out who wants to be notified of what and, using the project schedule, estimate when each person will need to be notified.

Table 5.1   Estimate of the Number of E-mails Generated over a Given Period

Steps in the Integrated Communication Strategy	Number of E-mails Generated	When
1. Updated tasks for a project are sent out by the project manager on the first Monday of the month to the team leader.	1	Week 1
2. The team leader then distributes tasks out to the team members by Tuesday morning with each team member receiving one e-mail to them that contains all task information. No-one else is cc'd or bcc'd into those e-mails.	5	Week 1
3. Team members should use chat or ad hoc conversations between themselves to achieve further clarification on the tasks. However, team members should not forward e-mails to each other with the task information and questions.	0	Week 1
4. If questions still remain, team members must submit all questions by Friday morning; all questions must be in one e-mail sent directly to the team leader without any cc's or bcc's.	0–5	Week 1
5. The team leader must send out a single response to all questions by the following Thursday directly to the team member who asked each question. If the team leader doesn't know the answer to the questions, they should call the project manager on Tuesday for a detailed question-and-answer session conducted over the phone.	0–5	Week 2
6. If team members still have questions, a meeting should take place on that Friday with the team members that have questions, the team leader and the project manager. No notes need to be generated from the meeting. The outcome is the project team having sufficient information to work on the tasks.	0	Week 2
7. If there are questions the project manager cannot answer, the task is pushed off for the following month's updated list while the project manager obtains the necessary information.	0	Week 2
8. The team members work on their tasks for the remainder of the month and report the status of their tasks at the end of the month with one e-mail each directly to the team leader without any cc's or bcc's.	5	Week 4
9. The team leader sends the project manager a single e-mail updating the status of all tasks, without any cc's or bcc's.	1	Week 4

Let's continue with our example of an environment with the well-defined communication strategy which we are using from Chapter 1. We can sum up the expected number of e-mails for each week as follows:

   ✓   Week 1: 11 e-mails. There are a possible 6–11 e-mails. Let's assume every team member has questions, so we estimate 11 e-mails for week one.

   ✓   Week 2: 5 e-mails. We are maintaining our assumption that every team member has questions and therefore the team leader needs to send 5 e-mails in week two.

   ✓   Week 3: 0 e-mails. Everyone is busy working. Ongoing communication takes place using other methods.

   ✓   Week 4: 6 e-mails. Each of the five team members sends an update to the team leader. The team leader sends one update to the project manager.

We can combine the number of expected e-mails for each week with a performance management baseline. Figure 5.1 shows communication integrated with a PMB. For purposes of this example, we are assuming that estimated cost, schedule and planned value have already been determined.

We can now collect data on the actual communication versus expected communication and compare it to performance management metrics to learn about the performance of the Project Environment. Here are a few potential scenarios.

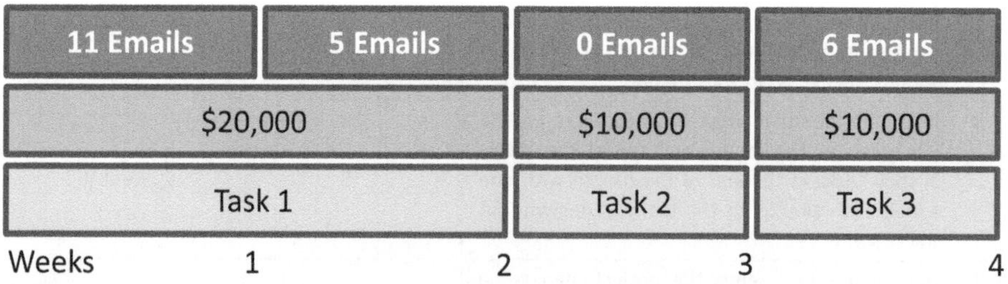

11 Emails	5 Emails	0 Emails	6 Emails
$20,000		$10,000	$10,000
Task 1		Task 2	Task 3

| Weeks | 1 | 2 | 3 | 4 |

Figure 5.1   Communication Integrated with a PMB

Our integrated baseline tells us that at the end of two weeks, we expect to complete Task 1 and earn $20,000 worth of value. This is accomplished with 16 e-mails in the environment. Let's discuss one scenario where we receive a status update that states that Task 1 is not complete even at the end of week four and that 16 e-mails were in the environment during the first two weeks. Communication went as planned, but we are behind schedule.

One possible conclusion is that the communication during the first two weeks was not clear. Team members did not understand the task and were not able to figure out what to do on their own. A potential path toward resolution is to investigate how the project manager or team leader expressed the task information. We can also look at how the team asked for clarification and how the team leader provided answers to their questions. There may be a disconnect between how the team phrased its questions and how the team leader responded. In such instances, effort can be made to facilitate more effective communication between the team and the team leader, such as constructing boundary objects.

Here is a second scenario, scenario two, representing a different Project Environment. We receive a status update that states that Task 1 is not complete even at the end of week four and that 11 e-mails were in the environment during the first two weeks. Communication is less than planned and we are behind schedule. Further analysis shows that 11 e-mails were in the environment in week one and 0 e-mails were in the environment in week two. A potential path toward resolution is to investigate why there weren't any e-mails in week two. We can see whether the team leader was responsive to the team's requests for more information—perhaps the team leader ignored the team's request for clarification.

Alternatively, consider a third scenario, based on the second scenario, where the team leader had other items to attend to and could only get back to the team during week three. If this were the case, this would show up in further analysis of the data. There would be 11 e-mails in week one, 0 e-mails in week two but 5 e-mails in week three. Let's call this scenario three.

The data provides insight into potential communication issues in the environment. This approach gives us a view into communication as a driver of project performance when analyzing and managing our projects. Schedule underperformance may reflect communication issues, for example, rather than technical issues. The communication metrics give us an indication of an environment's ability to recover from schedule underperformance and the potential cost of getting back on track.

We can express performance measurement and deviations in a format familiar to EVM practitioners:

- *Planned Communication (P COM)* = the amount of communication planned, or scheduled, to take place in a particular period of time. In our example above, P COM for the first two weeks is 16 e-mails.

- *Actual Communication (A COM)* = the actual amount of communication that took place in a particular period of time. In the first scenario above, where actual communication was in line with planned communication for the first two weeks, this would be 16 e-mails. In the second scenario, where 11 e-mails were in the Communication Environment during the first two weeks, A COM for the first two weeks would be 11 e-mails.

Table 5.2 shows P COM and A COM for the three scenarios discussed above. P COM and A COM are shown as cumulative values.

- *Communication Variance (COM V)* = the variance between actual communication and planned communication for a particular period of time. It is A COM – P COM and is expressed in the unit of measurement of the communication.

Table 5.3 shows COM V for each of the three scenarios at specific points in time.

Table 5.2   Cumulative Values of P COM and A COM for Scenarios One, Two and Three

	Scenario One		Scenario Two		Scenario Three	
Week	P COM	A COM	P COM	A COM	P COM	A COM
1	11	11	11	11	11	11
2	16	16	16	11	16	11
3	16	16	16	11	16	16
4	22	22	22	17	22	22

Table 5.3   COM V for Each of the Three Scenarios at Specific Points in Time

	Scenario One	Scenario Two	Scenario Three
Week	**COM V**	**COM V**	**COM V**
1	0	0	0
2	0	-5	-5
3	0	-5	0
4	0	-5	0

Here is how to read the table:

- For the first scenario, at two weeks COM V = 0. A COM = 16. P COM = 16. A COM – P COM = 0.

- For the second scenario, at two weeks COM V = -5. A COM = 11. P COM = 16. A COM – P COM = -5.

- For the third scenario, at two weeks COM V = -5. A COM = 11. P COM = 16. A COM – P COM = -5.

Interpreting the Data: Understanding People in the Environment

A zero variance indicates the environment has as much communication as anticipated according to the plan. A positive variance indicates that there is more communication in the environment than anticipated, while a negative variance indicates that there is less communication in the environment than anticipated.

However, a negative variance alone does not mean there is a problem with the environment—it means that the amount of communication is less than planned. To interpret the data, we need to compare it to other performance management data, such as schedule performance. In the second scenario, COM V is -5 and the project is behind schedule. In this scenario, negative variance indicates a problem; it helps us locate and fix the problem.

However, had the project been on schedule, the negative variance would have indicated that the environment required less communication than planned to complete the work on schedule. This could be because the team was more efficient at communicating than we thought or because the team figured things out themselves, let the team leader know that no additional communications were needed and therefore the team leader didn't need to send out five additional e-mails. This would be a welcome surprise. The combination of COM V and schedule performance indicates that the team and leadership exhibit behaviors that foster desired performance characteristics. We could investigate what made the team work effectively and try to replicate the design decisions of that Communication Environment in other environments. We would try to do the same were the project ahead of schedule and showing a negative COM V. Positive COM V values are interpreted in the same manner. The interpretation depends on its value relative to other project performance metrics.

The purpose of expressing communication as EVM-type metrics is to integrate communication as a Performance Management Tool into the lexicon and method of EVM practitioners and managers. Communication is a fundamental driver of project performance. Expressing communication in an EVM-type format raises awareness of communication and facilitates its use by EVM-oriented environments as a Performance Management Tool. It also offers another way of explaining the impact of communication on an environment's Solution Delivery Capabilities. The EVM-type metrics can trigger a deeper analysis of a Communication Environment to understand what is driving that environment's performance. It allows us to conduct root cause analysis on performance drivers, improve our forecasts of future performance and manage issues that affect project performance.

Take, for example, scenarios two and three in the above discussion. In both scenarios the project is late and there was a deficit of five e-mails at the end of week two. However, in scenario two, this deficit remained at the end of week four. In scenario three, the deficit was made up in week three. We can look deeper into the performance of COM V in the two scenarios.

Figures 5.2 and 5.3 show P COM and A COM for scenarios two and three.

As these figures demonstrate, COM V in both scenarios is -5 at week two, but COM V remains at -5 at the end of week four in scenario two, while in scenario three, COM V returns to 0 at the end of week four.

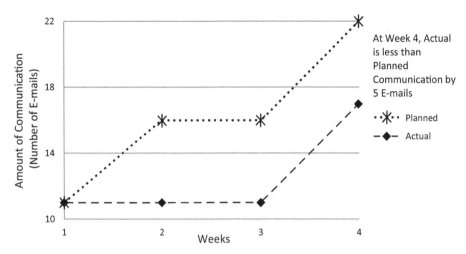

Figure 5.2   P COM and A COM for Scenario Two

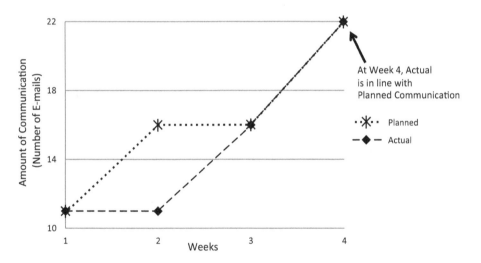

Figure 5.3   P COM and A COM for Scenario Three

We can start our root cause analysis with the observation of COM V in the environments. The causes of COM V are different in the environments represented by the two scenarios. In scenario two, the team leader did not reply to the team's e-mails in week two as planned. In fact, four weeks into the project, the team leader still had not responded to the team's e-mails. In scenario three, the team leader did not reply to the team's e-mails in week two as planned; however, they caught up with the communications and responded the following week. By the end of week four, actual communication was back in line with planned communication.

Using the observations of COM V, we can develop a hypothesis about the people in the Project Environment and their behavior. Based on the COM V observations in the two scenarios, we will focus our analysis on the team leader, since the team leader was expected to send the e-mails in week two. It is the team leader who did not respond to the team's e-mails in scenario two and who caught up with the team's e-mails in scenario three. Here are a few hypotheses about the team leader which we can develop based on the observation of COM V in scenario two:

- The team leader pushed-off the e-mails from the team, hoping to address them at a later date, but was not able to respond by week four.

- The team leader ignored the e-mails.

- The team leader forgot about the e-mails.

- The team leader communicated in other ways with the team.

- The team leader had to take care of other items and was not able to get back to the team by week four.

The data supports all of these hypotheses. It shows that the team leader did not communicate as intended at the planned time and never caught up on the communication by week four.

Here are few hypothesis about the team leader which we can develop based on the observation of COM V in scenario three:

- The team leader pushed-off the e-mails from the team and was able to address them by week four.

- The team leader initially ignored the e-mails, but came back to them later.

- The team leader forgot about the e-mails, but remembered them later.

- The team leader communicated with the team in other ways, then sent the e-mails as well at a later date.

- The team leader had to take care of other items and was able to get back to the team by week four.

The data supports all of these hypotheses. It shows that the team leader did not communicate as intended at the planned time, but did catch up on the communication by week four. Based on these hypotheses, we can arrive at the following conclusions about the team leader.

In scenario two, there may be many explanations for the team leader's behavior, but the data shows that, barring extenuating circumstances, the team leader is not aligned with the communication plan. The communication plan is a byproduct of management; it is a prescribed process for the Project Environment. Being unaligned with the communication plan may indicate that the team leader is not aligned with management or the prescribed processes of the Project Environment. The team leader is also not aligned with the team in the way described by the communication plan.

In scenario three, there may be many explanations for the team leader's behavior, but the data shows that, barring extenuating circumstances, the team leader may be late sometimes, but is aligned with the communication plan. This indicates that the team leader is probably aligned with management or the prescribed processes of the Project Environment. Also, the team leader may be late sometimes, but is aligned with the team in the way described by the communication plan.

Forecasting Future Performance

We can apply these conclusions to improve our forecast of project performance. Using our example, in both scenarios the project is late at the end of week four. We can use our conclusions to assess the probability of the two projects getting back on schedule, what it would take to get back on schedule and the estimated costs of doing so.

While in both scenarios communication is off plan at week two, scenario two has a COM V of -5 at the end of week four—it has remained off plan. We concluded that, barring extenuating circumstances, this is the case because the team leader is not aligned with one or more of the following: management, the prescribed processes of the Project Environment and the project team.

Scenario three has a COM V of 0 at the end of week four—it has gotten back on plan. We concluded that, barring extenuating circumstances, this is the case because the team leader is aligned with one or more of the following: management, the prescribed processes of the Project Environment and the project team.

The team leader from scenario three may be late, but eventually works back to plan; the team leader from scenario two does not.

Forecasting out, a Project Environment with the team leader from scenario three has a greater likelihood of getting back on schedule than a Project Environment with the team leader from scenario two. A Project Environment with the team leader from scenario three has a greater likelihood of getting all the planned work done and delivering planned outcomes than an environment with the team leader from scenario two. Anticipated deviations from the plan are higher in an environment with the team leader from scenario two. This may mean higher costs and even a replanning effort in that environment before the desired work gets done.

The forecast is based on using the conclusions about people's behavior in the environment, namely the team leader, as an indicator of that person's tendency to conform to the plan on which the project delivery schedule is based. The team leader in scenario three has shown a greater tendency to conform to the plan than the team leader in scenario two. The tendency of the leaders to conform to the communication plan may also indicate their respective alignment with the operating assumptions behind the project delivery schedule. For example, the team leader in scenario three and the person who put together the project delivery schedule share the same assumptions of how people in the project delivery team get information, share knowledge and solve problems, while the team leader in scenario two may have different assumptions.

The accuracy of the differing assumptions would manifest itself in the eventual performance of the Project Environment. For example, say the Project Environment ends up pulling the tasks back on schedule, but continued to show a negative COM V. This would happen because the team leader found a different way of getting things done; they changed the integrated communication strategy. They strayed from the pre-defined, approved communication strategy and used a different method to get the delivery team to accomplish the work of the project. Knowing this can help us to isolate which Communication Design elements or communication object elements were changed that led to the result obtained by the team leader in scenario two. This would be especially interesting if the Project Environment kept COM V at zero by the end of the project, but was off schedule. This would suggest that the operating assumptions behind the planned communication were not as effective as those used by the team leader who went off plan.

SPOTLIGHT: EARLY INDICATOR OF PERSONALITY AND SOCIAL ISSUES

In the preceding analysis, we compared COM V to schedule performance metrics and also cost implications. We can compare COM V to a multitude of project performance metrics and desired project capabilities, for example, team morale/team dynamics. There are many potential explanations for the team leaders' actions in the two scenarios. For example, in scenario two, if the team leader pushed-off the e-mails, they could be prioritizing other items ahead of the team, such as a different project or communication with a stakeholder. Perhaps the team leader is bad at managing their own time or perhaps they are hoping the team figures out how to solve the problem on their own or by going around them. They may go so far as to hold the team accountable for solving the problem, despite not responding to the team's e-mails. By using communication as a Performance Management Tool, we can get an early warning on potential leadership, personality conflicts and group dynamic issues that may reduce the likelihood of the Project Environment delivering the desired outcomes.

Ripple Effects: Second- and Third-Order Implications

Communication design decisions such as controlling the number of e-mails have ripple effects and impact project performance. As an example, let's explore the ripple effects of how the number of e-mails in the above example can affect project performance. By limiting the number of e-mails, we impact people's behavior, the way they communicate and the overall Communication Environment. While the number of e-mails does not directly control schedule performance, the Communication Environment does directly impact project performance. By limiting the number of e-mails sent, people will receive fewer e-mails overall. As we saw above in Chapter 3, the total amount of communication received is a variable that affects how people treat each discrete communication object they receive. The more communication they receive, the less impact each discrete communication object has, so the perceived value of each additional e-mail goes down while the amount of work required for each e-mail goes up. Each e-mail creates more noise for them to filter through and prioritize.

Further, limiting who may talk to who and the number of e-mails each person can send to each other may force the sender to spend more time constructing the e-mail and deciding whether it is necessary to use e-mail. They may be able to solve the problem themselves without sending the e-mail. This allows recipients to work with less interruption and spend more time focused on their specific task rather than filtering through e-mails. Limiting e-mails among team members may encourage them to talk to each other or use less formal methods of communication. This can foster increased collaboration, knowledge sharing and enhance opportunities for new knowledge creation within the team. The number of e-mails does not directly control schedule performance, but as a Communication Design decision that changes the Communication Environment, it does directly impact project performance.

This is not to suggest that the number of e-mails in an environment directly controls schedule performance. We can, however, use it as an indicator of how people behave on the project. Variance from the baseline can be a surveillance metric indicating that things aren't going according to plan with the Project Environment. As an indicator of social behavior, deviations from planned communication indicate that something may not be as expected in the underlying relationship between people in the environment or in the behavior of a group or individual. This can be a holistic metric used to gauge the overall health of your environment. It can also allow you to focus on where the problem might be and which design or object elements should be changed to improve the situation. For example, in the above scenarios, we can ask the following questions about people in the environment: are they being clear in their communications and are they being responsive?

The forecasted outcomes of the Project Environments in the two scenarios come from the interplay between the design of the Project Environment and the people in the Project Environment. The team leader in scenario two is not aligned with the design of the environment. There is a mismatch between the two. This team leader may excel in a different environment or the environment needs to change to accommodate the team leader. If we choose to change the environment to accommodate the team leader, we can look at the range of design decisions and communication object elements as items to change. We can make the changes and track their impact to see which changes give us the Solution Delivery Capabilities desired for the Project Environment. Communication as a Performance Management Tool can help us manage individuals and tailor Project Environments to capitalize on the behavior of the people we have in our environment.

The behavioral generalizations made in the scenarios are based on a limited data set. We only considered four weeks' worth of data. We can increase our understanding of the team leader's behavior with more data. We can also enhance our understanding of the drivers of the team leader's behavior by analyzing the relationship between elements of the Communication Environment and observable project behaviors over time. We can then use this enhanced understanding to better manage the team leader and therefore the project's performance.

In these scenarios, using communication as a Performance Management Tool provides additional insights into project performance and the environment's Solution Delivery Capabilities. It does so earlier than a system that relies on monitoring schedule and budget metrics alone. For example, a traditional EVM system would have shown scenarios two and three as having the same performance metrics. The forecast schedule and cost would be the same. And, importantly, the range of potential management actions we could take to improve forecast performance would be the same. However, as our analysis has shown, the root cause of the performance is different in the two scenarios and thus the management actions we can take to change performance will be different.

What it Means for Us

Communication can be an analytically rigorous and informative Performance Management Tool. We can use communication as a Performance Management Tool to understand, measure and manage people's behavior in a Project Environment. People's behavior drives project performance. Thus, we can better understand, measure and manage project performance using communication as a Performance Management Tool.

Communication can be integrated with existing Performance Management Tools such as EVM and put into a PMB. Alternatively, communication can be used independent of EVM. We can use communication as a Performance Management Tool to uncover the root cause of project performance and underlying behaviors that impact project performance, such as how responsive managers are, how well people are communicating, how well information is being conveyed and whether people in a Project Environment are on the same page with respect to critical assumptions such as framing assumptions and the way problems are being solved. The data from this analysis can improve our forecast of future project performance and facilitate better management decisions for attaining desired project outcomes.

6

A Checklist for Using Communication as a Performance Management Tool

Table 6.1 describes the approach for using communication as a performance management tool. It describes the technique using three different dimensions of description: conceptual, tactical and measurable. Conceptual describes the general concept of the process, tactical describes the tactics to turn the concept into action and measurable describes the tactical in terms of a measurable metric that can be analyzed and improved.

The table can be read both down one dimension and down and across the different dimensions. Reading the table down provides a description of the technique in three different ways. Reading the table down and across provides a description of the technique and a flow of how the technique can be implemented into a specific set of metrics. Steps 1–3 entail understanding the environment. Step 4 entails setting a goal and expressing the goal in terms of communication. Step 5 entails selecting which communication variables to use to achieve the desired goal. Finally, Step 6 entails execution—it is where the communication variables selected in Step 5 are utilized to achieve the goals set in Step 4. Step 6 includes iterative cycles of evaluating the results, making modifications and honing in on the goal.

The table is followed by a checklist describing the development and use of a specific application of the formal method, linking communication and project performance. Use it to develop the types of metrics discussed in Chapter 5. It also provides guidance on how to manage project performance using these types of metrics. Areas of further expansion on the technique are provided in parenthesis in the checklist and are prefaced with the word "Extension." The extensions also provide a deeper window into the theoretical assumptions behind the technique and they discuss areas where the technique can be tailored and expanded.

Table 6.1   Using Communication as a Performance Management Tool

Conceptual	Tactical	Measurable
Step 1 Understand the *Communication Environment* of your Project Environment.	a. Identify the elements of *Communication Design* in your environment.	i. Analyze your Project Environment to identify the *elements of Communication Design*.
		ii. Translate these elements into *measurable observations*.
	b. Identify the elements of *Communication Objects* in your environment.	i. Apply analytic tools to Communication Objects to derive *Communication Object Elements*.
		ii. Translate these elements into *measurable observations*.
Step 2 Understand the *observable behaviors* of your Project Environment.	a. Identify the current *Solution Delivery Capabilities*.	i. Analyze your Project Environment to identify the current *Solution Delivery Capabilities*.
		ii. Translate these capabilities into *measurable observations*.
	b. Identify the *current outcomes* of your Project Environment.	i. Analyze your Project Environment to identify the *current outcomes* produced by your Project Environment.
		ii. Translate these outcomes into *measurable observations*.
Step 3 Understand the *relationship* between the Communication Environment and the observable behaviors of the Project Environment.	a. Identify the relationship between elements of *Communication Design and observable behaviors* of the Project Environment.	i. Utilize *measurable observations* over time.
	b. Identify the relationship between elements of *Communication Objects and observable behaviors* of the project.	i. Utilize *measurable observations* over time.
Step 4 Identify *desired observable behaviors* for the Project Environment. These are the performance goals.	a. Identify the *desired Solution Delivery Capabilities*.	i. Identify the *desired Solution Delivery Capabilities*.
		ii. Translate these desired capabilities into *measurable observations*. This is what attaining the performance goal looks like, expressed in terms of the measurable observation which corresponds to the desired Solution Delivery Capability.
	b. Identify the *desired outcomes*.	i. Identify the *desired outcomes* for your Project Environment.
		ii. Translate these desired outcomes into *measurable observations*. This is what attaining the performance goal looks like, expressed in terms of the measurable observation which corresponds to the desired Solution Delivery Capability.

Table 6.1   Using Communication as a Performance Management Tool
               (concluded)

Conceptual	Tactical	Measurable
Step 5 Select *communication elements to use* to achieve desired project behaviors in the Project Environment.	a. Select elements based on the *understanding from Step 3.*	i. Which elements can help achieve *desired Solution Delivery Capabilities.*
		ii. Which elements can help achieve *desired outcomes.*
	b. Select elements based on *what you can measure, monitor and change.* Understand your span of control and *focus on those elements you can impact.*	i. Which elements can help achieve *desired Solution Delivery Capabilities.*
		ii. Which elements can help achieve *desired outcomes.*
	c. Select elements based on *additional analysis and understanding.*	i. Which elements can help achieve *desired Solution Delivery Capabilities.*
		ii. Which elements can help achieve *desired outcomes.*
Step 6 Use the selected elements to *achieve the desired project behaviors* for the Project Environment.	a. *Design, plan, execute, control and manage* Project Environments using these elements.	
	b. *Generate data* on the selected communication elements and achievement of the desired project behaviors.	
	c. *Interpret the data and make changes* to elements to select elements which can help achieve desired project behaviors.	i. This may require *changing the Project Environment.*
		ii. This may require *managing specific people* or *changing elements* to work with specific people and groups.
	d. *Iterate the process* to help achieve the target observable behavior and desired outcomes.	

A Checklist for Developing and Using the Type of Metric Described in Chapter 5

1.   Develop an integrated communication strategy as a baseline of planned communication in the Project Environment.   ☐

   a) Define the unit of measurement for communication. This is generally the y-axis of a graph of performance management. In the example above we used number of e-mails. Below, we generalize the unit of measurement to a Measurable Communication Action (MCA).   ☐

      i) Is that unit of measurement valid given the communication methods used in the Project Environment and other Communication Design decisions?   ☐

      ii) Is that unit of measurement an accurate reflection of the target observable behavior you want for your Project Environment? □

    b) Define a relevant corresponding variable to track against the unit of measurement for communication. This is generally the x-axis of a graph of performance management. In the example above we used time. We did this since we were tracking the relationship between the schedule performance of tasks over time and communication over time. (*Extension*: this can be generalized to other variables depending on the integrated communication strategy and the hypothesis of communication which you are tracking. For example, this could be phases of a project, in which case you would track planned communication against the phase of a project, such as how much effective communication there is during the initiation phase of a project, the requirements gathering phase, the execution phase, etc. Alternatively, you could track against the stages of team formation, such as planned communication when the team is forming, storming, norming, etc.) □

      i) Is that unit of measurement valid given the communication methods used in the Project Environment and other Communication Design decisions? □

      ii) Is that unit of measurement an accurate reflection of the target observable behavior you want for your Project Environment? □

2.   Develop an integrated baseline strategy for the planned target observable behavior and the desired outcome you want for the Project Environment. □

    a) Define the unit of measurement for the target observable behavior and outcome. This is generally the y-axis of a graph of performance management. In the previous example we used task completion. (*Extension*: task completion is dollarized in an EVM system to derive a dollarized value of planned tasks and compare this against the dollarized value of actual tasks and the actual cost of planned tasks.)   ☐

    i) Is that unit of measurement valid given the tracking systems in place in the Project Environment?   ☐

    ii) Is that unit of measurement an accurate reflection of the target observable behavior you want for your Project Environment?   ☐

b) Define a relevant corresponding variable to track against the unit of measurement for target observable behavior and outcome. This is generally the x-axis of a graph of performance management. This should be the same x-axis variable as that defined for tracking communication. (*Extension*: using the same x-axis variable, as it were, allows us to overlay communication measurement against a target behavior or outcome metric and establish a hypothesis of the relationship between communication, on the one hand, and performance of the Project Environment relative to the target behavior or outcome metric, on the other hand. In the example above we used time. We did this since we were tracking the relationship between the schedule performance of tasks over time and communication over time. Our hypothesis was that communication is directly connected to task completion over time. And this communication, as defined by the integrated communication strategy, describes how people should communicate in order to complete the tasks. This can be generalized to other variables depending on the target observable behavior or desired outcome and hypothesis of communication which you are tracking. For example, this could be phases of a project, in which case you would track planned communication against the phase of a project. The hypothesis would be that communication is directly connected to the phase of a project. And that communication, as defined by the integrated communication strategy, describes how people should communicate during each phase of the project. For further study, this can be linked together with other metrics such as schedule performance or cost performance to see how planned communication changes the schedule or cost performance of each phase.) ☐

    i) Is that unit of measurement the same as that used for the baseline of planned communication? ☐

    ii) Is that unit of measurement valid given the tracking systems in place in the Project Environment? ☐

    iii) Is that unit of measurement an accurate reflection of the target observable behavior you want for your Project Environment? ☐

3.   Combine the baseline of planned communication and the baseline of planned target observable behavior and the outcome for your Project Environment. (*Extension*: in our examples we have been doing this using a two-dimensional chart, such as tracking the schedule of planned communication against the schedule of planned task delivery. For further study, a larger set of variables can be used, combined and studied to develop multi-dimensional models linking communication and project performance.) ☐

4.   Track actual communication and actual achievement of target observable behavior and desired outcomes. ☐

5.   Analyze and interpret the actual data. ☐

a) Calculate the COM V between A COM and P COM. ☐

b) Calculate the variance of Project Environment performance between planned observable behavior, including desired outcomes, and actual observable behavior, including desired outcomes. ☐

c) Apply other analytic tools. ☐

d) Interpret the variances and data. ☐

e) Identify Communication Environment variables that can be changed, if necessary, to enhance the likelihood that the Project Environment exhibits the target observable behavior and increase the likelihood of delivering desired outcomes.   ☐

6.   Take management action, if necessary, by changing the relevant Communication Environment variables identified in the analysis and interpretation of the actual data.   ☐

7.   Iterate the process of tracking, analyzing, interpreting and taking management action to help achieve the target observable behavior and desired outcomes.   ☐

8.   Change the integrated communication strategy when necessary.   ☐

The Benefits of Using Communication as a Performance Management Tool

UNCOVER THE ROOT CAUSE OF PROJECT PERFORMANCE

Whether the full formal method or only portions of it are used, using communication as a Performance Management Tool has many advantages. First and foremost, it draws attention to the people and social aspect of a Project Environment. People's behavior directly impacts project performance. The Communication Environment helps us understand the social environment and human behaviors in the overall Project Environment, which directly impact an environment's Solution Delivery Capabilities and the likelihood that it delivers desired outcomes. As in our example above, we described the impact of the behavior of team leaders on project performance. We used our analysis of the team leader's behavior to forecast future performance of the Project Environment and derive management actions we could take to impact future performance.

Explicitly spelling out aspects of the Communication Environment reveals the underlying operating assumptions of how we think people should work together. It tells us about the Communication Environment and the impact our design decisions have on people's behavior and the Solution Delivery Capabilities of a Project Environment. It also provides an early warning into people-based factors that impact project outcomes before they are manifest in traditional metrics such as cost, schedule or technical performance. It can be used to capture a wide range of behaviors and object elements that may impact Solution Delivery Capabilities. Further, it provides us with direct insight into people and how they work together, which is the essence of how projects deliver desired outcomes.

BASED ON OBSERVABLE AND MEASURABLE PHENOMENA

This approach is based on observable and measurable phenomena, it is applicable to any Project Environment and doesn't rely on people mastering "soft skills" to improve communication (as is the case with other approaches to communication in business). With this approach, we can improve communication using observable and measurable elements of the Communication Environment and their relationship to observable behaviors of the Project Environment, such as specific Solution Delivery Capabilities and desired outcomes. We establish a chain of observable and measurable elements that together allow us to understand a Communication Environment and the component parts that can be changed to improve project outcomes.

This is analogous to the approach used in economics of Revealed Preferences, which says that we can understand people and their environment by observing the choices they make. For example, take a shopper who has the choice between two dishwashing detergents that are exact in every way, including price, except that one has a plain blue box and the other has a bright pink box with a gold star saying "new and improved." If this shopper chooses the detergent with the bright pink box and the gold star, we can assume they prefer that packaging over the plain blue packaging. This choice is observable and measurable. Economists use this information to uncover other factors besides price, quantity and quality that affect a person's decision-making process. Retail marketers and package designers use this kind of data to understand how to sell more of their products. We, as managers, can use this kind of approach to improve our projects.

APPLICABLE TO ANY PROJECT ENVIRONMENT

We can apply this approach to any Project Environment. We don't have to be subject-matter experts in a domain to improve communication on a project that involves that domain. This is analogous to quality approaches such as Six Sigma. A Quality Engineer trained in Six Sigma can use the same approach, tools and techniques on an aircraft manufacturing process as they use on a drug production process—the approach is applicable across domains.

NO NEED TO MASTER SOFT SKILLS

Because it is based on observable and measurable phenomena, this approach doesn't require the traditional soft skills-based training that pervades the discussion on communication in business. Rather, it replaces it with an analytic method. It doesn't ask people to change who they are or how they behave, it asks people to use available data to make informed design and management decisions.

SPOTLIGHT: ANALYZE LIKE GOOGLE DOES

Google makes money on advertisements when somebody clicks on an ad which Google displays to them. For that reason, Google continually develops algorithms to learn which ads it should display to any particular person. The better the fit between the person and the ad, the more likely it is that that person will click on the ad and the more money Google makes.

Google uses observable and measurable data to match people and ads. This data includes the words people use in their searches, the words used in the advertisement, how many other people have clicked on that ad, what ads someone has clicked on before, the website someone is on, the website they just came from, videos they may have just watched, the device they are on and their location.

Google's ad-serving algorithms learn about each person by the choices they make online. They don't rely on understanding the "meaning" of the words someone uses or the intent of their choices, they abstract from the content itself and maximize the informational value of those observable choices. Google uses this approach whether the ad is for a dry-cleaning service or for a new car. It seeks to use all available information to maximize the fit between the person and the ad, with the goal of getting the person to click on the ad. Google doesn't "know" somebody, it only knows the data around that person, but that is more than enough information for it to make good matches between the person and the ads it shows them.

In the same way, communication can be used as a Performance Management Tool by using observable and available data to find the right fit between the people in the Project Environment, on the one hand, and the Communication Objects and Communication Design elements, on the other hand. The right fit is when the Project Environment exhibits the specific Solution Delivery Capabilities needed to deliver the desired outcomes. With Google, the right fit is attaining the maximum clicks for the ads that it shows.

Considerations When Using the Formal Technique

UNIQUENESS OF EVERY ENVIRONMENT

The relationship between an element and the use of the object varies according to the Project Environment, the project participants, technology and goal. It is important to understand the relationship between the Communication Environment and observable behaviors for your Project Environment. For example, we can't generalize what time of day it is best to send out a communication—it depends on what action we are trying to accomplish and what technology we are using. Above, in the example of time of day, we saw that the hours of 3 pm to 5 pm featured the highest level of retweets. If our goal is retweets, the hours between 3 pm and 5 pm seem to be best. However, when looking at CTRs for e-mails in the graph (Figure 6.1, based on Zarella's studies), we see that those hours represented nearly the lowest average CTR. If our goal is CTRs and we are using e-mail, those are precisely the wrong times to send the communication.

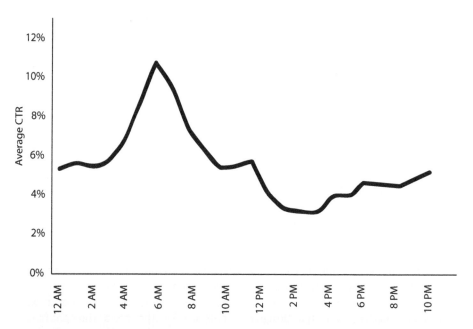

Figure 6.1   CTRs by Hour

Source: Reproduced from *Zarrella's Hierarchy of Contagiousness*, The Domino Project, August 2013 with the kind permission of Seth Godin.

Uniqueness by Project Environment is a common trait across other project management activities. For example, there is no single general sequence of tasks in a project; each network diagram is the result of project specific constraints. Similarly, there is no single general set of task durations or of an overall project schedule; each set of task durations or schedules is affected by a variety of factors. However, despite the fact that there is no single rule, we can sequence tasks, determine durations and create project schedules. We do this by applying generally accepted techniques to work to create a network diagram. We can then apply generally accepted techniques and tools to the network diagram to determine task duration and ultimately a project schedule. We have adopted the same approach here, describing guidelines and considerations to account for when using communication as a Performance Management Tool.

As we gather data on the relationship between specific elements of a Communication Environment and the observable behavior of a Project Environment, we can build up an institutional repository of knowledge on these relationships. This repository can become an organizational asset and guide for best practices within the organization. It can be used to help people design, plan, control and manage Project Environments to produce desired Solution Delivery Capabilities and desired outcomes.

UNIT OF ACCOUNTING

In environments that can and want to measure multiple communication elements, it is efficient to create a single unit of measurement for communication. For example, let's say we want to add the amount of chat that goes on in the Project Environment to our metric above. We could define the communication elements and design decisions that constitute the chat we are allowing and measuring in our environment, and we could estimate the amount of chat for each week. We would then combine this with the number of e-mails each week. This would create a single unit of measurement for communication.

In past presentations I have referred to this unit of measurement as an MCA. It can be made up of a single method of communication or multiple methods of communication. The methods can be added together, giving all methods equal weight, or different methods can be weighted when combining them into an MCA. The weighting can reflect variables such as the relative value management places on each form of communication or the strictness with which Communication Design decisions are enforced for each method of communication. It can reflect the phase of the project or the expected activities for that period of time. It can also be tweaked to increase sensitivity toward one method of communication over another to facilitate management awareness of unpredicted behavior. For example, in our sample project in Chapter 5, chat could be heavily weighted in weeks one and two so that any actual chat in the environment would quickly generate deviance from the baseline and flag an unpredicted behavior for the Project Environment. When using MCAs, the label for the unit of measurement for expected communication in Figures 5.2 and 5.3 (the graphs showing P COM and A COM for scenarios two and three) would change to MCAs instead of number of e-mails. The formulae would change into the following expressions:

- *Planned Communication (P COM)* = the amount of communication planned, or scheduled, to take place in a particular period of time, expressed in terms of MCAs.

- *Actual Communication (A COM)* = the actual amount of communication that took place in a particular period of time, expressed in terms of MCAs.

- *Communication Variance (COM V)* = the variance between actual communication and planned communication for a particular period of time. It is A COM – P COM and is expressed in terms of MCAs.

These expressions are more generalizable. They account for any method of communication and allow for tailoring the metric to measure particular concerns. However, it does abstract the unit of measurement for communication from the design decisions such as the method of communication and how strictly the use of any method is enforced. These design decisions determine what communication is valid for measurement and therefore what communication is included in the metric. This added level of abstraction can lead to confusion when first introducing communication as a Performance Management Tool.

I've referred to this combined measure as an action to highlight that we can make conscious and active decisions about communication. Further, action places the responsibility for crafting the communication in the hands of the sender. It is up to the sender to be aware of how their communication may be received by the recipient because it is the recipient who determines the importance of any particular communication. As the common saying goes, what matters is what the hearer hears, not what the sayer says—or communication is truly in the eyes of the receiver.

Accounting for the Method of Communication and Technology Choices

The methods of communication used in a Project Environment determine the objects created. Thus, it determines the object elements which we can study and the way people can use the objects. The methods of communication determine what we can observe and study. We can only ask questions that the environment can answer. For example, we can study the open rate of an e-mail to see how many people cared about the content of the e-mail enough to open it. However, we cannot study the open rate of in-person meeting attendance. Therefore, it is important to align the methods used in an environment with the kind of analyses we'd like to undertake on an environment.

List of Common Communication Methods

Here is a list of common communication methods. The list is separated into technology-based methods and traditional methods. Since we are using communication to manage project performance, the methods of communication used in a Project Environment determine the design and object elements with which we can manage project performance. The variables available to us to improve project performance are directly connected to the methods of communication used in the environment. We can only manage elements and behaviors that exist in the environment and which are observable. For example, we can manage the number of in-person meetings held in an environment that uses meetings, but we cannot manage the number of in-person meetings held in an environment that doesn't use in-person meetings as a method of communication.

Technology-Based Methods	Traditional Methods
➢ E-mail	➢ In-Person Meeting
➢ Chat/Instant Message	➢ Phone Call
➢ Project Website	➢ Conference Call
➢ Twitter	➢ In-Person Conversation
➢ Google Doc	➢ Paper Documents
➢ Message Board	
➢ Wiki	
➢ Webinar/Web Meeting	
➢ VOIP Call	
➢ Video Conference	

The use of technology is growing as the primary method for communicating. The technology choices we make for conducting communication determine the Communication Objects created; thus, it determines the observable elements of that object which we can study. It also determines how that object can be used by someone and therefore the observable behaviors we can study. For example, e-mail creates an electronic artifact that has observable elements such as from, to, cc, bcc, subject, body text (which can be further analyzed using semantic analysis tools), links, images, attachments, time stamp, date stamp and size. Observable behaviors with the object are opening it, clicking on a link, clicking on an image, forwarding it and replying to it. This range of elements and observable behaviors defines the types of analysis we can conduct with e-mail.

Attaching documents to an e-mail provides a different set of observable and measurable events from attaching a link. For example, we can track open rates on an e-mail to which the documents were attached, but we cannot easily track whether the documents were opened or shared with others. However, adding documents to an e-mail as links to another site provides observable events, such as how often the link was clicked on and whether other people besides the recipient of the e-mail clicked on the lick, in addition to the open rates. We can also track when the link was clicked, how often it was clicked, what type of device the person was using when they clicked on the link (a PC or mobile device, for example) and potentially where they were physically located when they clicked on the link. Thus, if we wanted to track how relevant the documents were to the recipient, the data available to derive conclusions varies according to the technology choices we make.

Similarly, using e-mail compared to a tool like Twitter provides a different set of observable and measurable events. For example, someone can send an e-mail to any recipient without the recipient's permission—all the sender needs is the recipient's e-mail address. With Twitter, however, the recipient decides who they want to hear from. They do this by subscribing to receive tweets from that sender. And if the recipient wants to stop receiving information from that sender, they can unsubscribe from that sender. Thus, if we wanted to track how relevant a recipient finds information from a sender, the data available is different between e-mail and Twitter.

CATALOG OF ANALYTIC AND MANAGEMENT PARAMETERS FOR COMMUNICATION METHODS

Table 6.2 illustrates a sample cataloging of the analytic and management parameters for a few communication methods. The catalog shows the

Communication Objects produced by that method, Communication Object elements for that object and observable behaviors for that object. This list is intended to illustrate how to look at communication methods so that we can align the choice of methods with what we can learn about that environment and what we can manage in that environment. Though not expressly listed, many of these technologies are able to create logs of the objects. This approach of aligning communication methods with what we want to learn about the environment is not limited to technology-based communication methods. Traditional, non-technology-based communication methods also create Communication Objects that have Communication Object elements and observable behaviors. We have included a sample cataloging of a meeting as an example of a non-technology-based communication methods, the objects it creates, the object elements and observable behaviors.

Table 6.2   A Sample Cataloging of the Analytical and Management Parameters for Several Communication Methods

E-mail			
Communication Objects Created			
➢ E-mails			
Common Communication Object Elements			
➢ From	➢ To	➢ Cc	➢ Bcc
➢ Subject	➢ Body text	➢ Links	➢ Images
➢ Attachments	➢ Time stamp	➢ Date stamp	➢ Day of the week
➢ Message size			
Observable Behaviors with the Object			
➢ Opening it	➢ Clicking on a link	➢ Clicking on an image	➢ Forwarding it
➢ Reply to sender	➢ Reply to all		

Chat/Instant Message			
Communication Objects Created			
➢ Chat messages			
Common Communication Object Elements			
➢ Sender	➢ Recipient	➢ Message text	➢ Links
➢ Images	➢ Files sent	➢ Time stamp	➢ Date stamp
➢ Day of the week	➢ Time between responses		
Observable Behaviors with the Object			
➢ Replying to it	➢ Clicking on a link	➢ Clicking on an image	➢ Downloading a file

Table 6.2   A Sample Cataloging of the Analytical and Management Parameters for Several Communication Methods *(concluded)*

Project Website			
Communication Objects Created			
➢ A project website			
Common Communication Object Elements			
➢ Information design	➢ Navigation	➢ Button placement	➢ Search options
➢ Images	➢ Website text	➢ Number of pages	➢ Device compatibility
➢ Findability	➢ Links from other sites	➢ Links to other sites	➢ Internal links
➢ Number of forms	➢ Form design	➢ Privacy Statement	➢ Pop-ups
➢ Other content on site	➢ Security warnings	➢ Advertisements on site	➢ Terms and conditions
Observable Behaviors with the Object			
➢ People's path on the site	➢ Entry page	➢ Exit page	➢ Bounce rate on site
➢ Where people were before the site	➢ Where people went from the site	➢ Search terms used to find the site	➢ CTR for links on the site
➢ Views by content	➢ Location of visitor	➢ Device of visitor	➢ Number of unique visits
➢ Number of repeat visitors		➢ The full array of web analytics	

Twitter			
Communication Objects Created			
➢ Tweets			
Common Communication Object Elements			
➢ The Tweeter	➢ Number of followers on the account	➢ Retweets	➢ @replies
➢ Hashtags	➢ Tweet text	➢ Links	➢ App used to Tweet
➢ Time stamp	➢ Date stamp	➢ Day of the week	
Observable Behaviors with the Object			
➢ Retweet	➢ Subscribe to account	➢ Unsubscribe from account	➢ @reply

Meeting			
Communication Objects Created			
➢ Meeting invite	➢ Meeting agenda	➢ Meeting notes	➢ Action items
Common Communication Object Elements			
➢ People invited	➢ Length of invite	➢ Word choice in invite	➢ Invite sender
➢ How far in advanced it was scheduled	➢ Length of meeting	➢ Length of agenda	➢ Word choice in agenda
➢ Meeting location	➢ Length of notes	➢ When notes are distributed	➢ Word choice in action items
Observable Behaviors with the Object			
➢ People attend	➢ People decline	➢ Forward the invite	➢ Read the agenda
➢ Propose changes to agenda	➢ Forward the invite	➢ Read the notes	➢ Propose changes to notes
➢ Forward the notes	➢ Read the action items	➢ Work on the action items	➢ Forward the action items

---

SPOTLIGHT: MORE WAYS OF COMMUNICATING IS NOT ALWAYS BETTER

When surveying seminar participants about the impact communication technology has had on their organizations, the vast majority say that technology has hurt communication within their organizations. Methods of communication have proliferated without rules or guidance on how to use them and what they should be used for. This causes a diffusion of where conversations take place, making it harder for people to share knowledge about a task or to collaborate together to create new knowledge about a task.

Introducing more methods of communication is not always better for a Project Environment. It limits the span of influence that communication management can have as a Performance Management Tool and reduces the benefits that better communication can have on an environment. Increasing the number of communication methods can adversely affect an environment's Solution Delivery Capabilities.

STRICTNESS IN CONTROLLING METHODS OF COMMUNICATION

Some environments are stricter than others when it comes to the methods that can be used for communication. Some may allow anybody to use whatever method they would like, but others may more tightly control the tools that people can use. The degree of strictness impacts how tightly we can connect Communication Object elements and design elements with observable behaviors. For example, we can manage the number of e-mails people send as a Performance Management Tool in environments that require people to use e-mail for all communication. In environments that allow people to use e-mail, chat, text and message boards for all communication, it is more difficult to focus on the number of e-mails people send as a Performance Management Tool.

This same consideration comes into play when looking at the design decision of defining the method for specific subject-matter domains. Some environments are stricter when it comes to defining the communication methods that can be used for specific subject-matter domains. For example, some specify that all technical support questions have to be carried out using an online technical support portal, while others allow people to contact customer support using any method they wish, such as e-mail, phone call, instant message, in-person meetings and an online technical support portal.

The degree of strictness impacts how tightly we can connect Communication Object elements and design elements with observable behaviors in that domain. For example, we can manage response time on the online portal as a tool for managing performance of a technical support group in environments that limit technical support communication to an online portal. In environments that allow people to communicate with technical support using a wide variety of methods, it is more difficult to use response time on an online portal as a tool for managing performance of a technical support group.

What it Means for Us

In this chapter we have extended the formal technique for using communication as a Performance Management Tool by introducing a checklist for building communication metrics for Project Performance Management. In Chapters 5 and 6 we have discussed the benefits of the formal technique and shown how it can help us directly manage the root cause of project performance: people. We have shown that it does not require the soft skills or domain level knowledge of traditional communication management techniques. We have argued that it is robust and scalable, and we have demonstrated how it can provide indicators of performance issues earlier than traditional performance management techniques, and can point the way to management action that can be taken to get the project back on track.

We have discussed items to consider when setting up and using communication as a Performance Management Tool. Like all Performance Management Tools, the value of the tool depends on how we set up the system, interpret the data generated by the tool and use the data to design, execute and manage our Project Environments. However, even without full implementation, communication can be used as a valuable Performance Management Tool.

The enhanced awareness of the role that communication plays in determining project outcomes makes us better system designers, planners, managers and leaders, regardless of whether we implement or utilize the formal technique or not. The enhanced awareness pushes us to focus on the driver of project performance, which is people operating in the social environment of a Project Environment. Thus, using communication as a Performance Management Tool allows us to align the Performance Management Tool set with the nature of the underlying reality of project performance.

If project performance is driven by people, shouldn't we use performance tools that are oriented toward people?

To conclude Part I of the book, let's summarize the key things to take away. Communication environments directly impact an environment's Solution Delivery Capabilities and the likelihood that it will deliver the desired outcomes. The design of a Communication Environment is made up of various design elements. These are the choices we make, or the facts on the ground we have to live with, about the Communication Environment. Whether we can change the design or not, we can improve project performance by being aware of the design of the Communication Environment we operate in.

Communication Objects are the way we communicate. They are artifacts created by the communication methods we use and are a function of the design of the Communication Environment. As such, studying Communication Objects helps us to understand the design of the Communication Environment and how the environment impacts people's behaviors.

However, a Communication Object is more than the informational content of the artifact. We can apply analytic tools to the object to derive different elements of the Communication Object. These elements are descriptors or non-informational content-related characteristics of the object. People's behavior relative to a Communication Object is impacted by the Communication Object elements of that object. We can change how people use the object by changing the object elements. Since Communication Objects and object elements are a function of the design of the Communication Environment, we can study the relationship between people's behavior and Communication Objects to understand the Communication Environment.

The behavior of a Project Environment is the aggregate of the actions people take in the environment. We expanded on the relationship between observable elements of the Communication Environment and people's behavior. We argued that there is an observable relationship between the observable elements of a Communication Environment and the observable behaviors of a Project Environment. Based on this, we proposed the use of communication as a Performance Management Tool.

We then described an approach for using communication as a Performance Management Tool. The approach includes measuring communication, creating a baseline of communication, tracking communication, analyzing data about communication and interpreting the data in order to enhance our design, management and leadership decisions. We spelled out the approach in a checklist that formalizes the technique of using communication as a Performance Management Tool. We then discussed items to consider when designing a system that uses communication for performance management. We concluded with an argument on the importance of using communication as a Performance Management Tool since it addresses the underlying driver of project performance, namely, people.

In Part II we will continue with the final argument made here on the importance of using tools that address the underlying nature of what our goals are on a project. In the case of Project Environment behaviors and outcomes, we have argued that since the underlying nature of the performance is people in a social environment, we should use communication as a Performance Management Tool.

Part II deals extensively with the subject of properly aligning the tools we use with the underlying nature of what it is we are trying to use them for. It takes the understanding of the role people play in project outcomes to another level and argues for further considerations we need to take into account when designing, planning, executing, managing and leading Project Environments. Specifically, we will argue that it is critically important to accurately understand the nature of uncertainty in Project Environments. Uncertainty, we will argue, stems directly from people, human decision making and human choice. The decision-making processes and choices people make are impacted directly by the project's Communication Environment. Thus, getting the Communication Environment right is not only important for project performance but also for creating a Project Environment that can accurately address the underlying challenges facing any organization in today's competitive environment.

PART II
Communication Manages Project Complexity

7

Orientation Toward Uncertainty

Uncertainty is one of the defining factors of a project. It differentiates a project from a standardized process and from ongoing operations. Project environments differ in their orientation toward uncertainty. A Project Environment's orientation toward uncertainty impacts the solutions delivered by that Project Environment. Environments oriented to work with a high degree of uncertainty produce different outcomes for a given set of circumstances from those which are oriented to work with certainty.

Orientation toward uncertainty is different from risk tolerance. Risk tolerance assumes that all risks can at some point be identified, quantified and managed for a given cost. The potential impact of all risks on a project can be summed and presented to stakeholders. Risk tolerance is a gage of how much risk stakeholders are willing to bear on that project. Stakeholders with a high risk tolerance will spend less money on reducing the potential impact of risks than stakeholders with a low risk tolerance. Stakeholders with a low tolerance for risk will spend money and resources reducing the potential impact of risks. Risk tolerance is a threshold level. This is different from orientation toward uncertainty.

Orientation toward uncertainty is a design element of a Project Environment. It describes how an environment is designed to react to uncertainty and it is based on the perception, by Project Environment Participants, of how great a role uncertainty plays in the Project Environment. Environments where the prevailing view is that everything is under control or can be controlled react differently to uncertainty compared to environments that admit a low level of control over the factors of a Project Environment. Consequently, environments that believe everything can be controlled produce different outcomes from those that admit a low level of control. Environments where people believe they can have a high level of control have different Solution Delivery Capabilities from those that admit a low level of control.

Orientation toward uncertainty can be described using the topology of tame, messy and wicked. This topology was introduced by Hancock and Holt to categorize risks. It describes the source of uncertainty of a risk and how to manage that uncertainty. We will apply this topology to an environment's orientation toward uncertainty.

Tame risks are those which can be managed by describing the uncertainty with sufficient detail to develop a solution to the uncertainty. For example, a broken toilet can be fixed by investigating the source of the problem, describing the source of the problem and solving the problem. The source of uncertainty on a tame problem is coming up with a sufficient description of the problem itself. Messy risks can be managed in much the same way as tame risks; however, there is additional uncertainty in integrating multiple components that may have competing impacts. For example, building a car with good gas mileage can be achieved by making a car out of a lightweight material. However, the material has to be strong enough to meet government crash safety standards. For a messy problem, uncertainty is compounded by having many components working together. The source of uncertainty in a messy problem lies in understanding the interrelationship between all components and the overall system. Both tame and messy problems can essentially be addressed by getting the right technical experts and "working the problem." The probability distribution of outcomes for Project Environments dealing with tame and messy uncertainty narrows the more experts know and understand the uncertainty. Given sufficient analysis and understanding, the probability distribution will converge to one single outcome.

Wicked problems are entirely different—they are managed by managing people. The sources of uncertainty in wicked problems are people's decision-making processes and the actions they decide to take. Unlike tame and messy problems, wicked problems cannot be "worked." There is no amount of expertise which can applied to a wicked problem to come up with a solution that all participants will agree on.

Take climate change, for example. Some people believe it exists and is caused by human actions, while other people believe that it does not exist or that, if it does, it is not caused by human actions. Both sides have experts that have analyzed and "worked" the problem. However, no amount of experts or data will bring the two sides to an agreement on whether anything needs to be done about it and, if so, what should be done. In order for either side to implement its approach to climate change, the other side must be managed. This requires leadership and management skills rather than technical expertise.

Wicked problems are addressed by getting everyone to agree on a path forward. The probability distribution of outcomes for Project Environments dealing with wickedness narrows as Project Environment Participants are driven to accept a specific solution. This can come from consensus building or other forcing mechanisms for getting a group to accept a solution. However, it is important to clarify that the distribution of outcomes for Project Environments dealing with wickedness does not necessarily narrow the more experts know and understand the uncertainty. The likely outcomes of a Project Environment can stay widely dispersed and include a wide range of outcomes even after decades of research and debate.

We can use this topology to describe perceptions toward uncertainty. Some people perceive all uncertainty as being tame or messy and do not recognize wickedness. They believe that all uncertainty can be dealt with by breaking down the problem to component parts, solving the problem at the component level and then putting it all back together. The difference between someone who perceives uncertainty as tame versus messy is the amount of complexity admitted in taking a problem apart and putting it back together. Incidentally, this is the type of uncertainty which caused the outcome in the Mars Orbiter case study mentioned earlier. Some people, on the other hand, recognize wickedness. They believe that there is always some element to a problem which cannot be solved by "working the problem."

These perceptions impact an environment's orientation toward uncertainty. The perceptions allow us to understand how an environment is designed to react to uncertainty and allows us to predict how an environment will react toward it. Take an environment which is oriented to handle all uncertainty as tame or wicked: when uncertainty comes, participants will obtain technical specialists and assign the specialists to work the problem, whereas when an environment which is oriented to account for wickedness encounters uncertainty, participants will look to each other to work through the uncertainty.

The risk workshops that took place in relation to Heathrow Terminal 5 highlight the differences in orientation toward uncertainty. The 1996 workshop assumed that uncertainty could be managed and set about implementing a tame and messy approach to managing uncertainty. The project was broken down into six subprojects. Technical experts, engineers and accountants were brought in to identify all potential risks and develop risk management plans for risks identified in these subprojects. The risk management plans relied on each technical expert performing their functions independently or only as prescribed by the technical interrelatedness of the work on the project.

The 2000 workshop assumed that there was uncertainty that could not be managed and set about implementing an approach to managing wicked uncertainty. The project was dealt with as a whole rather than being broken down into subprojects. Leaders from different participant groups were brought in to discuss overall uncertainty on the project and identify ways that participant groups could work together to manage uncertainty on the project when it appeared. The risk management plans relied on people working together to address uncertainty and develop relationships that would facilitate managing that uncertainty.

This was driven by introducing the idea of "respecting the last possible moment" for decision making. This opened the door to accepting the high degree of uncertainty inherent in the endeavor, or, to quote from the Hancock and Holt paper:

> The inclusion of last responsible moment meant the framing of the risk workshop changed from an emphasis upon delivering problem-solution coefficients to articulating those practices that afforded the project team the greatest space for reflection upon the nature of the problems they faced, before having to take a decision. This emphasis upon reflection and conversation meant it was considered critical to choose the participants based on their influence and ability to explore prevailing and emerging business issues.[1]

The relationship between an environment's orientation toward uncertainty and its Solution Delivery Capabilities is more than a matter of recognizing wickedness—it is a matter of matching a problem with the right problem-solving methods. Environments which accurately match problem-solving methods to problems produce different outcomes from those that don't. Hancock and Holt attribute the success of Heathrow Terminal 5 to accurately matching the approach to uncertainty adopted by the Project Environment with the reality of the situation. The reality is that there was a high degree of wickedness in the

---

1   Hancock and Holt, "Tame, Messy and Wicked Problems in Risk Management," p. 15.

Project Environment. The biggest potential source for problems on the project was neither technical difficulty nor contract-related issues—it was interpersonal relationships. Thus, the Project Environment improved its ability to deliver a solution that addressed this uncertainty by adopting problem-solving methods that recognized wickedness. The Project Environment was designed to handle wicked uncertainty.

In contrast, Hancock and Holt point to the 1994 collapse of the Heathrow Express tunnel as evidence of a mismatch between a problem and the problem-solving methods applied to solve it. The Heathrow Express tunnel followed traditional risk management practices, which assumed that all risks are tame or messy. Following standard practice, technical experts identified the risks, planned risk responses and developed risk management plans. Unfortunately, despite being the state-of-the-art method for risk management, it was not sufficient to guarantee the desired outcome—in 1994 the tunnel collapsed. This is an example of a mismatch between the problem-solving methods applied to solve a problem and the problem itself. The Project Environment was not oriented to handle wicked uncertainty.

Leadership of the F/A-18 E/F was oriented to handle wicked uncertainty. This was done by creating an environment of trust and visibility that included all Project Environment Participants, such as the contractors performing the work, members of the government who wanted the work done and members of the government who allocated the money to fund the work. Within this environment, no-one was surprised when there were surprises. The environment was oriented toward wicked uncertainty; it could manage surprises across all project participants and therefore work together to move through surprises.

The people behind the Fold.it website created an environment that invites wicked uncertainty. The environment makes it easy for new people to work with the problem and develop solutions that can be used by specialists. Fold.it leverages wicked uncertainty by opening the door to a diverse set of people who can solve the problem. The X-Prize Foundation embraces wicked uncertainty in a similar manner to drive desired outcomes. It capitalizes on wicked uncertainty by opening the door to a wide range of problem-solving methods and welcomes a wide range of solutions to the problem. These environments deliver the desired outcomes because they recognize the unavoidable existence of wicked uncertainty. They are designed to work within the presence of wicked uncertainty as opposed to reducing or ignoring wicked uncertainty.

These examples highlight the relationship between an environment's orientation toward uncertainty and its Solution Delivery Capabilities.

Observable Manifestations of Orientation Toward Uncertainty

An environment's orientation toward uncertainty manifests itself in the observable behaviors of the Project Environment. The observable behaviors impact an environment's Solution Delivery Capabilities. Environments that are oriented toward tame and messy uncertainty have different Solution Delivery Capabilities from those oriented toward wicked uncertainty.

FLEXIBILITY IN ORGANIZING TEAMS

Orientation toward uncertainty can manifest itself in the flexibility that managers have in organizing teams. Environments oriented to tame and messy uncertainty restrict flexibility. For example, managers must work with the teams they are assigned, regardless of the interpersonal dynamics of the project participants. The managers are expected to rely on process to determine project outcomes; they must adapt the people to the process.

A related element is where flexibility is constrained so that team members can only be chosen based on quantifiable characteristics. An example of this is an environment where managers choose team members based on skill set or seniority, regardless of the interpersonal dynamics of the project participants. The managers are expected to rely on process to determine outcomes. People are slotted into the process based on the quantifiable characteristic they possess. For example, any senior designer can fill the slot of senior designer prescribed by the environment's predefined processes.

Managers in environments oriented toward wicked uncertainty have greater flexibility in organizing teams. Managers can select the team members they would like to work with. They may do so based on non-quantifiable characteristics. They are expected to rely on the people they select to deliver the project outcomes, so they adapt the processes to allow people to deliver the desired outcomes.

Environments which restrict the flexibility of organizing teams have different Solution Delivery Capabilities from those which allow for greater flexibility. The Solution Delivery Capabilities of restricted environments depend on how well the Solution Delivery Process addresses the underlying problem. The Solution Delivery Capabilities of more flexible environments depend on how well the people on the team can solve the problem.

FLEXIBILITY IN ADAPTING PROCESSES

Orientation toward uncertainty can manifest itself in the flexibility that people have in adapting processes. Environments oriented to tame and messy uncertainty restrict flexibility. For example, managers must use pre-defined processes regardless of how the Project Environment is performing. The managers are expected to figure out how to implement the processes to produce the desired outcomes; they must adapt people, schedules and costs to the process.

Environments orientated toward wicked uncertainty have greater flexibility in adapting processes. Managers, for example, can change the processes as necessary to improve performance of the Project Environment. Team members, as another example, can self-organize, propose and implement new processes for delivering desired outcomes. The process is expected to adapt to project performance such as schedule and costs.

Environments which restrict flexibility in adapting processes have different Solution Delivery Capabilities from those which allow for greater flexibility. The Solution Delivery Capabilities of restricted environments depend on how well the Solution Delivery Processes address the underlying problem, attain the desired outcomes and project performance metrics. The Solution Delivery Capabilities of more flexible environments depend on how well the team can adapt processes to achieve the desired outcomes and performance metrics.

Environments that require project oversight face a potential challenge in allowing flexibility in process adaptation. Oversight is conducted by defining the performance metrics that the Project Environment must produce and report on. The processes for producing performance metrics are an additional layer on top of an environment's Solution Delivery Processes. These additional processes further impact an environment's Solution Delivery Capabilities. Project environments that restrict flexibility in terms of adapting the processes that produce performance metrics have different Solution Delivery Capabilities from those which allow for more flexibility in adapting the processes that produce performance metrics.

The challenge arises from the oversight requirement. Producing performance metrics is a required capability of the Project Environment. In some environments, like the F/A-18 E/F, the capability of producing performance metrics can be seamlessly integrated into the environment's overall Solution Delivery Capabilities. It does not impede the Project Environment's ability to attain the desired outcomes; in fact, it can facilitate the environment's performance by acting as a boundary object between the multiple groups in the environment. For example, in the F/A-18 E/F program, government program managers, contractors, engineers and government sponsors used the performance metrics as a single point of truth about the program. It facilitated clear communication and cleared the way for the task delivery teams to focus on delivering the desired project outcomes. Alternatively, in other environments, the capability of producing performance metrics becomes a hindrance to delivering the desired project outcomes.

RELIANCE ON PREDICTION

Orientation toward uncertainty can manifest itself in how deeply an environment's Solution Delivery Processes rely on prediction. Environments oriented toward tame and messy uncertainty rely on prediction. Those that rely on prediction produce different outcomes and have different Solution Delivery Capabilities from those that are less reliant on prediction. Those that rely heavily on prediction lock in the competitive trade-offs between scope, cost and schedule. Take, for example, instances where requirements documentation describes the solution to a problem well before people start working on solving the problem. The rest of the Solution Delivery Process flows down from the requirements documentation, which includes estimated cost and schedule. The requirements are a prediction about the future and there is a perceived causality between, on the one hand, scope and, on the other hand, cost and schedule. In these environments, new information learnt during the Solution Delivery Process is perceived as a challenge to the Solution Delivery Process and necessitates a re-evaluation of cost and schedule. Scope change is a prime example—it presents project participants with a re-evaluation of the budget and schedule. They are generally unwelcome, burdensome and costly in environments that rely heavily on prediction.

In contrast, environments that rely less heavily on prediction have greater freedom when considering the relationship of scope, cost and schedule. In these environments, it is assumed that new information will become available throughout the Solution Delivery Process. Requirements are viewed as a starting point for delivering a solution rather than a prediction. Decisions on cost and schedule can flow from sources other than the requirement documentation. There is no perceived causality in the Project Environment between scope and cost and schedule. For example, organizational politics may determine the project budget. Competitive pressures from the marketplace may determine the schedule. Scope changes do not necessitate a re-evaluation of cost and schedule. New information is perceived as beneficial to the Solution Delivery Process rather than a challenge to it.

An environment's reliance on prediction is connected to project participants' reliance on prediction and therefore participants' expectations. Expectations management has a different focus in environments that rely heavily on prediction compared to environments that rely less heavily on prediction. For example, in environments where cost and schedule flow from the requirements documentation, scope changes require managing expectations in relation to scope, cost and schedule. The manager must explain the scope change, its impact on the cost and schedule, and why the cost and schedule were not designed to accommodate the scope change ahead of time.

In contrast, in environments that rely less heavily on prediction, expectations management has less of a focus on explaining why something wasn't predicted and accounted for ahead of time. For example, when a scope change occurs in these environments, the manager does not have the sole responsibility for obtaining and justifying cost and schedule impacts. It is the manager's role to inform project participants about cost and schedule impacts; however, it is the environment's responsibility to decide and deliver cost and schedule impacts since cost and schedule flow from sources other than the requirements.

An environment's reliance on prediction is connected to the elements of flexibility in organizing teams and flexibility in adapting processes. Environments that rely heavily on prediction restrict the flexibility of managers and project participants to organize teams and adapt processes, while those that are less reliant on prediction allow for greater flexibility in terms of organizing teams and adapting processes.

Here is an example of these different factors at play. I was once asked to comment on a proposed volunteer policy for a non-profit organization. There were two competing approaches being proposed. The first approach required board members to list all volunteer positions which they would need for the coming year, have the positions and reporting structure for the volunteers approved by the board, and have the budget allocated to cover any costs related to the positions. The second approach allowed board members to create and fill volunteer positions on an ad hoc basis at their sole discretion. There were no pre-determined position descriptions or pre-defined processes for working with the volunteers and costs related to the position would be paid for out of the board member's already-approved annual budget.

The first proposed approach would encourage the board to spend time predicting, planning, discussing and lobbying for potential positions. Once the positions were voted on, board members would be constrained to filling those positions and working with volunteers only in the capacity in which they were approved. This approach relied heavily on prediction, but limited flexibility in organizing teams and flexibility in adapting processes. Prediction and discussion were used to identify all available volunteer needs ahead of time and how the volunteers would work to meet those needs. This approach had the benefit of transparency and oversight. It also allowed the board to brainstorm on needs for the coming year and to obtain input from the entire board.

However, this approach also constrained board members from filling needs that were not predicted or from working with volunteers in ways that were not previously predicted. It further constrained communication from the membership to the board. If a member had an idea that could help the organization and wanted to work on it, the member had to wait until the annual meeting to submit the idea for approval as a volunteer position. So, in addition to limiting flexibility in organizing teams and flexibility in adapting processes, this approach, based on a reliance on prediction, would impact the organization's Solution Delivery Capabilities. It would constrain the organization's ability to act quickly in response to potential opportunities and constrain where the organization looked for solutions and the range of solutions that it could consider.

The second approach would encourage board members to act entrepreneurially to find areas where volunteers could help and to capitalize on ideas that volunteers might have. Board members and volunteers could work together to determine the plan of action and a mutually agreed-upon way in which they would work together. Once the board member and the volunteer were in agreement, they could start to execute the plan. This approach did not rely on prediction and provided a high degree of flexibility in organizing teams and flexibility in adapting processes. Flexibility was used to identify volunteer needs as they arose and to define how volunteers would work to meet those needs on an ad hoc basis. This approach had the benefit of fostering entrepreneurship and independent action. Board members could act quickly to capitalize on potential opportunities, look for solutions across the entire membership and consider a wide range of solutions. It also saved time at the annual meeting since the board would not have to cover the topic of volunteers at the meeting.

However, this approach also limited transparency and oversight. The board was entrusting each individual board member to act in good faith and in concert with the organization's goals. Once the board member's annual budget was approved, they could act as they saw fit with respect to costs associated with a volunteer position. Further, it eliminated the opportunity for the board to brainstorm on needs for the coming year. In doing so, it eliminated an opportunity for the entire board to be in alignment on the organization's volunteer needs and how meeting those needs would contribute to attaining the organization's strategic goals. It constrained the amount of information the board member had to report to the board about the volunteer's activities and reduced the board's ability to oversee those activities. So, as consequence of increasing flexibility in organizing teams and flexibility in adapting processes, this proposed approach reduced the organization's ability to predict potential problems that could arise from the volunteer activities or a board member's work with a volunteer. It also reduced the board's ability to address potential problems ahead of time. The reduced ability to predict also reduced the ability to rely on prediction and take action in advance of potential problems.

At the time of writing, the board had not yet adopted a particular approach. A hybrid approach will likely be adopted that fosters entrepreneurship and independent action, but allows oversight by the board through reporting. This is a prediction based on an understanding of the people involved in the debate on the board. However, there is no clear optimal solution and no amount of analysis which can determine the right solution. The solution that is adopted will reflect the competing interests of the board members, the trust relationships among the board members and the design of the Communication Environment.

Here is another example, a hypothetical scenario, based on real-life circumstances, where the intentional lack of the ability to predict would force a change in flexibility in organizing teams and flexibility in adapting processes. The military sometimes needs to test equipment about which very little information is known ahead of time, such as that built in highly classified environments. There are two groups involved in testing: there is the group that built the equipment and there is the group that needs to design the test environment. There is no communication between the groups, except for conveying rudimentary technical information, such as the requirement for electrical power and scheduling information such as when the test should take place.

Traditionally, test environments are designed based on a test plan that tests the specific capabilities of the equipment being tested. The traditional approach uses a tame and messy-oriented approach to design and build the test environment. The test environment flows directly from information about the specific capabilities of the equipment being tested and specifically tests these capabilities. Operators for the environment are selected based on their ability to operate the test equipment and follow the test plan.

In a scenario of limited information, though, the test designers' first instincts would be to build a process, using an approach oriented toward tame and messy uncertainty, which could accommodate the unknowns. It would be based on an attempt to predict potential capabilities and an attempt to design an environment that could be flexible enough and broad enough to test whatever the designers predict would come up. The test environment would be a highly complicated, integrated system intended to account for a wide range of potential scenarios. However, it would not be flexible. A wide range of tests could be conducted that pieced together multiple components. However, ad hoc tests, which fell outside of predicted permutations, could not be conducted in that test environment. Left to the traditional approach, the test designers would tackle the lack of predictability by wrestling the unknown into a tame and messy framework. This would create a mismatch between the ability of the test environment to meet the needs of the underlying problem and would reduce the chance for the test environment to meet the testing needs. Further, the people chosen to operate the test would be determined by the need to operate the complicated test environment that would be built.

Rather, an approach oriented toward wicked uncertainty would be recommended. It best mirrors the nature of the uncertainty of the underlying problem and increases the chances of the test environment meeting the test needs. A tame and messy-oriented approach could work if the information about the equipment's capabilities were available; however, it was not.

The test designers should focus on people first. Since the uncertainty is wicked, the Solution Delivery Capabilities should be people-based. Finding the right person to operate the equipment should be the starting point to meet the testing needs. The right person can develop the test plan on the fly as they learn about the equipment's capabilities and the testing needs. They can adapt the test plan and the test environment to fit the testing needs. They can also provide a wide range of feedback, on questions both anticipated and unanticipated, that is based on their particular experience with the piece of equipment. This feedback will not be limited to observations required by the test plan. Since the test plan is adaptive, as is the environment, the observations may not conform to pre-defined expectations. They may or may not contribute to the specific questions which the testing was supposed to answer—it all depends on the person selected to test the piece of equipment. This risk, however, of getting all the required test data can be managed. The operator can be prepared ahead of time to answer specific questions such as "will operating this piece of equipment put my life at risk?" Knowing that they will be asked to answer this question, the operator can focus on creating a sufficient number of experiences that will allow them to answer it. So, a lack of ability to rely on prediction should result in a change in flexibility in organizing teams and flexibility in adapting processes in order to give the test environment the Solution Delivery Capabilities that could most likely meet the testing needs.

GAGING PROJECT PERFORMANCE

Reliance on Prediction can manifest itself in how project participants gage project performance. Environments oriented toward tame and messy uncertainty leverage the reliance on prediction and gage project performance using comparisons against predictions of performance. Environments that rely heavily on prediction develop performance measurement techniques based on variance from predicted performance. For example, EVM relies on a comparison of current project performance against a prediction of project performance called a performance measurement baseline (PMB). A project can perform better than the baseline (positive variance), worse than the baseline (negative variance) or in line with the baseline (zero variance). Variances from the baseline flag a potential performance issue, whether it is over-performance or underperformance.

Variances can be interpreted in different ways and are interpreted differently in environments that rely heavily on prediction compared to those that rely less heavily on prediction. Consider, for example, a spectrum of interpretations, depending on how heavily the environment relies on prediction. At one end of the spectrum with those that rely heavily on prediction, variances are interpreted as a result of how people are performing on the project. At the other end are those that don't rely on prediction at all, where variances are interpreted as a result of the unpredictability of forecast project performance. Most environments fall somewhere between the two ends of the spectrum.

The interpretation of performance data impacts the type of corrective measures managers take to change project performance and the environments they design. Environments oriented toward tame and messy uncertainty leverage performance measurements based on comparisons against predictions and employ techniques to bring performance into line with the prediction. For example, managers in an environment that relies heavily on prediction will react to a variance signifying underperformance through corrective measures to change people's behavior on the project. Managers will encourage people to alter their behavior in a way that moves the project performance data back toward the baseline. They will design environments that focus on utilizing incentive structures to maintain the baseline. At the other extreme, managers in an environment that doesn't rely on prediction will react to a variance signifying underperformance through measures that encourage a re-evaluation of the baseline. They will design environments that focus on utilizing variances to flag the appearance of new information about the Project Environment that can be used to change project performance. They will also employ techniques to bring performance into line with an updated picture of the desired outcome.

The 2000 risk workshop from Heathrow Terminal 5 is a good example of designing an environment that seeks new information and integrates it into the Solution Delivery Process. This was accomplished by focusing on "respecting the last responsible moment of decision making." Decisions were not made ahead of time. There wasn't a list of expected observations in project performance that would trigger a pre-decided set of actions as a response; rather, decisions were pushed-off until the last responsible moment. Responses could be tailored based on the most up-to-date information and could be carried out by whichever participants were in the best position to deal with the situation, as opposed to having pre-determined roles of who should carry out a pre-decided set of responses.

VISIBILITY INTO THE ENVIRONMENT

Orientation toward uncertainty can manifest itself in how much visibility participants have into the market space in which they operate and how they interpret what they see in that space. Environments that are oriented toward tame and messy uncertainty pre-define the types of observations available and the interpretation of those observations. This limits visibility to observations that have been pre-determined to be relevant and also limits the interpretation of those observations to a pre-defined set of interpretations. An environment's Solution Delivery Capabilities will change depending on how well the pre-defined types of observations and interpretations match what is really going on in the market space.

Environments that are oriented toward wicked uncertainty allow for unexpected observations and develop interpretations that fit the observations. This expands visibility into the environment and expands the number of potential interpretations. An environment's Solution Delivery Capabilities will change depending on how well participants can focus on relevant observations and develop interpretations that match what is really going on in the market space.

We have seen numerous examples of organizations that have been affected by not having accurate visibility in the market space. For example, recently we have seen the demise of Kodak in the face of digital photography, Borders Books when challenged by electronic books and Dell Computers' move to privatization in the face of the market's shift to tablets, phones and other non-PC computing devices. There are also classic examples like Xerox, which couldn't capitalize on the PC revolution despite having developed its foundation, or the US Postal Service, which is under constant pressure from overnight delivery services (such as FedEx, UPS and DHL) and the declining use of physical mail. These organizations were not able to accurately see and interpret changes in the market space and this limitation constrained the actions they were able to take. All information fed into a stagnant interpretation until the market rendered its final judgment.

In contrast, some firms, like Microsoft, have consistently been able to accurately recognize shifts in the market and willing to re-direct efforts to capitalize on these shifts. They have been open to seeing new observations, flexible in the interpretations of the observations and willing to maneuver to take advantage of the shifts in the marketplace.

Take, for example, Microsoft's response to the Internet. In a 1995 confidential internal memo to Microsoft's Executive Staff and direct reports,[2] Bill Gates

---

2   "The Internet Tidal Wave" by Bill Gates, 26 May 1995, made public as a result of the US Department of Justice's trial against Microsoft. Available at: http://www.usdoj.gov/atr/cases/exhibits/20.pdf.

described how the Internet will change everything: "The Internet is the most important single development to come along since the IBM PC was introduced in 1981." He listed the changes the Internet would bring and was unafraid to compare the Internet to the company's internal products: "Amazingly it is easier to find information on the Web than it is to find information on the Microsoft Corporate Networks. This inversion where a public network solves a problem better than a private network is quite stunning."

Gates directed all business units to incorporate the Internet into their plans and into their way of thinking, regardless of other projects that the business units might have been working on before. To quote the memo: "Now I assign the Internet the highest level of importance. In this memo I want to make clear that our focus on the Internet is critical to every part of our business." He followed this up by making changes in the organizational structure and setting strategic direction for business units so that the organization could respond to the shifts in the market. Within months, Microsoft began launching products to compete in the changed market space.

These observations and interpretations were not the product of an isolated visionary. Gates received information and interpretations from a variety of sources within the company. The company was structured to find new information, share that information, explore interpretations of this and collaboratively begin to develop solutions in response to the potential implications. It was oriented toward a high degree of uncertainty and fostered communication to work with the uncertainty. In the face of even greater uncertainty, the memo exhorted the organization to foster even greater communication: "There will be a lot of uncertainty as we first embrace the Internet and then extend it. Since the Internet is changing so rapidly we will have to revise our strategies from time to time and have better inter-group communication than ever before."

SPOTLIGHT: HOW VISIBILITY AND FLEXIBILITY HELPED US PILOTS TO WIN IN THE KOREAN WAR

Visibility and the flexibility to maneuver quickly were key reasons why US pilots beat North Korean pilots during the Korean War.[i] This was the conclusion of John Boyd's 1974 research and analysis of dogfights during the war. On paper, the

i   This story is based on anecdotal evidence cited in Captain William S. Angerman's, 2004 MS thesis at the Air Force Institute of Technology entitled "Coming Full Circle With Boyd's OODA

MiG-15s flown by the North Koreans should have won. In almost every measure, their planes were technically superior to the US F-86s. The North Koreans had the better hardware and the better technology, but in the air, the US pilots won.

Boyd noticed that while the North Korean planes had better all-round technology, the US planes had three advantages: they gave pilots a better view of the area around them; they could be maneuvered faster and better; and the US pilots were able to quickly adapt their tactics in the face of changing circumstances. Taken together, this meant that the F-86 pilots could see what was going on better, read the signs of what their adversary's next move would be and change their own position to be in a better position before the adversary knew what was going on. The US pilots would outflank the North Koreans and would be in a dominant position before the latter even knew what had hit them. As such, these elements gave the US pilots a competitive advantage.

Aerial dogfights are a two-person battle of communication. Every move a pilot makes communicates an intended tactic to the other pilot. The pilot who can most accurately understand the communication and decisively react to it wins. Visibility into the environment and flexibility to alter tactics are competitive advantages. If a pilot were locked into a limited view of the environment, they would be operating at a disadvantage. Were they constrained in the type of interpretations they could make of their adversary's moves, they would be at a disadvantage. And were they limited in the tactics that they could implement, they would be at a severe disadvantage.

The benefits gained from visibility and flexibility in this environment are proportional to the amount of wicked uncertainty in the environment. Were one pilot to unfalteringly follow a pre-defined set of actions, the competing pilot would simply have to design and implement a set of superior counter-actions. In this situation an orientation toward tame and messy uncertainty would match the operating environment and could deliver an appropriate solution. However, when pilots operate in environments of increased individualized decision making and unpredictable action, an orientation toward wicked uncertainty is more likely to deliver an appropriate solution. The same dynamic exists in every operating environment between the underlying nature of the uncertainty in the environment and the Project Environment's orientation toward uncertainty. Project environments that best match orientation toward uncertainty to the underlying nature of the uncertainty of the environment in which the project operates have a better chance of delivering a desired outcome.

Loop Ideas: An Analysis of Innovation Diffusion and Evolution," Air Force Institute of Technology, Department of the Airforce, Air University, AFIT/GIR/ENV/04M-1.

Resilience

Orientation toward uncertainty can manifest itself in how resilient an environment is to external changes. Environments that are oriented toward tame and messy uncertainty are resilient to the extent that the external change fits within the defined processes and Solution Delivery Capabilities of that environment. Changes that have not been thought of or that are of a different nature compared to those for which the processes were designed can stress the environment and break it.

Environments that are oriented toward wicked uncertainty are resilient to the extent that people in the environment can figure out a way to work together in the face of external changes. Changes necessitate flexibility among the participants. Relationships or people which are not able to be flexible in response to the changes can stress the Project Environment and break it.

What it Means for Us

We can combine the Observable Manifestations of orientation toward uncertainty with elements of the Communication Environment to enhance our analysis of the relationship between a Communication Environment and the observable behavior of a Project Environment. We can add the orientation toward uncertainty to our use of communication as a Performance Management Tool. This provides an even deeper analytic, management and control tool for designing environments for desired Solution Delivery Capabilities and for the increased likelihood of delivering the desired results.

Table 7.1 is a list of the Observable Manifestations of orientation toward uncertainty, combined with the list of the elements of Communication Objects and design elements in the Communication Environment. We can use this list to understand an environment's Solution Delivery Capabilities. This is a list of only these variables which we have previously discussed; there are other variables and observations which capture relevant characteristics of the Project Environment.

As you look at the list, you will notice overlap and interconnectedness among the variables. For example, there is a connection between the manifestation of orientation toward uncertainty of "Flexibility in Organizing

Teams" and the design element of "Organizing Teams." The decision on how to organize teams can be decentralized in an environment that offers flexibility in organizing teams, whereas the decision on how teams are organized is more centralized in environments that offer less flexibility in organizing teams.

Another example is how the format of the Communication Objects used to communicate project performance relates to the reliance on prediction and the way in which performance is gaged in the environment. This, in turn, relates to how task activity is described in a Project Environment. For example, environments that use EVM metrics to report project performance and have a heavy reliance on prediction limit the format of Communication Objects to the numerical representation of the EVM metrics, such as SPI = 0.85. This in turn limits the type of artifact used to describe task information in the Project Environment. It may be limited to a specific report format that contains the SPI information.

Table 7.1   Observable Manifestations of Orientation Toward Uncertainty

Manifestations of Orientation Toward Uncertainty	Elements of Communication Objects	Design Elements of the Communication Environment
➤ Flexibility in Organizing Teams ➤ Flexibility in Adapting Process ➤ Reliance on Prediction ➤ Gaging Project Performance ➤ Visibility into the Environment ➤ Resilience	➤ Time of Day ➤ Day of the Week ➤ How Much You Broadcast to an Audience ➤ Readability ➤ Emotional Tone ➤ Word Choice ➤ Audience Characteristics ➤ Total Quantity of Information a Person Receives ➤ Boundaries between Groups ➤ Is it a Boundary Object? ➤ The Process that Generates the Communication Object	➤ Organizing Teams ➤ Locating Teams ➤ Assigning Tasks ➤ Describing Task Information ➤ Coordinating Activity ➤ Who Can Talk to Who in a Project Environment ➤ Setting Rules for Each Method ➤ Defining the Method for Specific Subject-Matter Domains ➤ The Schedule of Communication ➤ The Workflow of Communication ➤ Communication Strategy

SPOTLIGHT: THE CONSTRAINTS OF AGILE ACQUISITION IMPLEMENTED BY THE US ARMY

The US Army has developed an evolving approach for testing and acquiring capabilities called the Network Integration Exercise (NIE) and the Agile Acquisition (AA) process. The desired outcome for the approach is to enhance the Army's ability to acquire and deliver the right equipment to soldiers at the right time and at the right price. The approach is set up as repeated and interconnected cycles of publishing requirements, selecting vendors and testing the vendors' equipment in high-fidelity, integrated test environments, the culmination of which is participation in the NIE.

With this approach, the Army's ability to deliver the right equipment is enhanced by testing the equipment in integrated environments to make sure it works with all the other gear a soldier possesses and by having many soldiers work with the equipment in highly realistic scenarios. The Army's ability to deliver the equipment at the right time is enhanced by wrapping the call for vendors around participation in a test process (the NIE) rather than around an acquisition event. Being selected to participate in the NIE does not mean that the technology has been selected to be acquired by the Army. The Army's ability to acquire equipment at the right price is enhanced by pushing the research and development risk onto the vendors, encouraging vendors to re-purpose existing technologies or find alternative markets for their technologies in order to amortize research and development costs over a number of customers. This relieves the Army of the responsibility of having to absorb these costs entirely through its acquisition of the technology and therefore reduces its costs.

Like all processes set up to attain desired outcomes, the NIE/AA process constrains the Project Environment. The process constrains the range of potential participants in the environment and the Solution Delivery Capabilities of the Project Environment. In this case, the Communication Design of the process limits the type of information available to potential vendors. For example, a potential vendor does not know if they will get a return on participating in the event or not, which constrains the range of potential participants. Small vendors with high-risk solutions will have a difficult time making a rational decision on whether to participate. In areas where more information is made available to potential vendors, it constrains the kinds of solutions that will be offered. For example, there is ample information on the technical requirements for potential solutions and on the model for having reduced acquisition costs. Potential vendors with solutions that are strictly for the Army will have a difficult time making a rational decision to participate. Similarly, vendors with solutions that the Army may want to keep out of the public sphere will have a difficult time making a rational decision to participate.

The NIE/AA is an evolving concept that will change over time. It is experimental and is meant to generate further information on ways to best meet the processes' goals. To find the right balance among non-convergent options of possible ways to structure the approach, leadership will likely account for feedback from project participants and further research being carried out into the process.

Taking the analysis a step further, there is a ripple effect in relation to whether the Communication Object, in this case the report on the SPI, is a boundary object. Does the report format facilitate communication between different groups? Whether it needs to or not is a function of object and design elements such as how the teams are organized, which determines if there are different groups, the flexibility of organizing teams, boundaries between groups and who can talk to who in a Project Environment.

Following this analysis, it becomes clear that there is no single solution set for the question. There is no one "right" answer; it all depends on what combination of decisions works best for the project participants. The solution that will be arrived at for the environment is the set of decisions which the project participants abide by. We, in our analysis, cannot determine a single solution set. However, we can understand the interconnectedness between these decisions and the Solution Delivery Capabilities of our environment. With this understanding in hand, we can make better decisions and manage environments toward specific Solution Delivery Capabilities, namely, those capabilities which generate the desired outcomes.

For example, we may want to design environments that consistently deliver projects on budget and on time, and which provide stakeholders with many oversight metrics. We can do that; however, it comes at a cost. This cost includes tightening the relationship between, on the one hand, the cost and the schedule, and, on the other hand, the scope, as well as tightening the relationship between, on the one hand, the number of groups involved and the boundaries between groups, and, on the other hand, the need to create boundary objects.

There is no single right answer for how we should structure our Project Environments or the elements we should use in our Communication Objects. This is true even if we identify a single desired set of Solution Delivery Capabilities. It all depends on the people involved. It is a wicked situation.

Further, by understanding the connections between the orientation toward uncertainty, object elements and design elements, on the one hand, and an environment's Solution Delivery Capabilities, on the other hand, we can better understand the implications that our desired outcomes have on other parts of the Project Environment. For example, choosing on budget, on time and lots of oversight as a desired outcome constrains the type of solutions that the delivery team can consider and therefore constrains the environment's Solution Delivery Capabilities. Each set of desired outcomes we choose constrains an environment's Solution Delivery Capabilities.

8

All Uncertainty is Wicked

As it turns out, all uncertainty on a project is wicked. Wicked uncertainty is uncertainty which does not have a single convergent solution set. It is a function of human behavior and is present in every Project Environment. But it is more than unavoidable; all uncertainty in a Project Environment is wicked uncertainty. Other sources of uncertainty, such as technical, environmental, financial or legal issues, only become problems when project participants change their behavior in response to an issue manifesting itself.

Take, for example, a construction project that uncovers an archeological artifact on the construction site. The impact of the find can be negligible or huge, depending on human behavior. The crew that finds the artifact has a choice as to whether to report the finding or not. Once reported, management has a choice as to whether to report the finding to the project sponsors or not. The project sponsors may or may not report the finding to the requisite authorities. And the authorities, once they receive a report on the find, may have a range of options to choose from in reaction to the finding, which may include anything from not caring that an artifact was found and letting construction proceed to shutting down the entire construction project until further archeological research is done on the site. At each step of the way, the impact of finding the artifact is completely dependent on human behavior.

Project Environments that are oriented toward only tame and messy uncertainty will have a mismatch between the underlying problem and the method for solving the problem. For example, an environment oriented toward tame and messy uncertainty may prescribe regulation as an answer to determining the outcome of finding an archeological artifact on a construction site. The regulation could state that all findings must be reported and must result in an immediate stop to all work until further archeological research is conducted. With regulation in place, therefore, we should be able to accurately predict the impact of finding an artifact at any point in the project lifecycle and develop accurate risk management plans to address it. However, the reality is that complying with regulation is still a matter of human behavior. The regulation, in this case, fails to address the underlying issue of human behavior and creates a false sense of predictability around the Project Environment.

On the other hand, Project Environments which are oriented toward wicked uncertainty have a better chance of accurately matching the problem-solving method with the problem. For example, an environment oriented toward wicked uncertainty may recognize that no matter how much regulation is in place, there may still be surprises that result from the discovery of an archeological artifact on a construction site. With this in mind, the environment will prepare itself to establish the relationships and ad hoc management decisions that may need to be made to respond to surprises.

To be clear, the fact that all uncertainty in a Project Environment is wicked does not eliminate the importance of other sources of uncertainty. Finding an archeological artifact can still be a problem for a Project Environment. However, the way the uncertainty is managed is impacted by an environment's orientation toward uncertainty. For example, in both cases above, there is a risk management plan in place to address the underlying issue of finding an artifact. However, in the environment oriented toward tame and messy uncertainty only, the risk management plan ends at the execution of plans that address all known issues. Participants' behavior is constrained and focused on their particular role in executing the predicted and discrete steps in the plan. In the environment orientated toward wicked uncertainty, the risk management plan has an open-ended component that expects ad hoc interaction between project participants and lays the groundwork for those interactions ahead of time. While other sources of uncertainty are still incredibly important, environments with an orientation toward wicked uncertainty have different Solution Delivery Capabilities from those that are only oriented toward tame or messy uncertainty.

To put it another way, the presence of wicked uncertainty is an extension of the constraints faced by all Project Environments. Projects are constrained and choices have to be made between scope, cost, schedule, quality and other factors such as stakeholder impact. For example, take a Project Environment that encounters a technical problem affecting the ability to deliver a solution that meets all of the desired requirements. Project participants can choose options such as keeping the same scope, increasing the budget and extending the schedule or they can choose to cancel the project because it won't meet all of the original requirements and they don't want to raise the budget or extend the schedule. There is no single "right" answer. Each outcome is a choice. Orienting an environment toward wicked uncertainty recognizes the role of human behavior when facing these choices and, moreover, the fact that people may have competing interests when making these choices.

This conclusion that all uncertainty is wicked is supported by recent research. Marcel Hertogh and Eddy Westerveld researched sources of complexity as part of their 2009 PhD thesis[1] at Erasmus University Rotterdam. Hertogh and Westerveld are practitioners on large infrastructure projects (LIPs). They carried out a detailed study on six LIPs from multiple countries with a combined value of over €20 billion in construction costs and projects lasting over 15 years when the planning and discussions that went into the project are included. They divided complexity into six different categories: technical, social, financial, organizational, legal and time complexity. They then asked practitioners: "What makes your project complex?" Overwhelmingly, social complexity was the most dominant form of complexity experienced by the practitioners asked. Technical and organizational complexity came in a distant, though still significant, second, followed by financial complexity. Time and legal complexity were the least mentioned sources of complexity.

As the authors state: "Social complexity is the dominant and central complexity within LIPs."[2] Digging deeper, they uncover the fact that other forms of complexity can be reduced to social complexity. Organizational, legal, technical or financial uncertainty only become problems on a project when they cause social complexity. To quote the study:

> *Our cases provide some interesting examples of these dynamics.*
> *For example the tunnel safety sub-case at the A73-South. Here the*
> *technical complexity, a new unproven technology, resulted in rising*
> *cost estimates. This in turn caused friction in the stakeholder network*
> *because it started a debate about who would pay for this increase. At the*
> *same time we see that the technical complexity made it unclear how the*
> *new CAF (or water-mist) technology would meet safety requirements.*
> *Again we see a relationship between technical complexity and social*
> *complexity. This seems easy to explain: problems do not arise when*

---

1   Marcel Hertogh and Eddy Westerveld, "Playing with Complexity—Management and Organisation of Large Infrastructure Projects," Erasmus University Rotterdam, 2010. I had the pleasure of learning about Eddy's research through his presentation at EVM Europe 2012 at the University of Twente, the Netherlands.

2   Ibid., p. 176.

there is no reason for any of the players to change behaviour in the
project. So the types of complexity really only cause trouble when they
influence the interests of stakeholders.[3]

This supports the assertion that all uncertainty is wicked.

What it Means for Us

Given that all uncertainty is wicked, we can improve our Solution Delivery
Capabilities by designing environments that account for wicked uncertainty.
As we saw in Chapter 1, Conway's Law tells us that solutions delivered by a
Project Environment mirror the Communication Structure of that environment.
Environments whose structure more accurately matches the underlying nature
of the problems they are trying to solve have a better chance of delivering
solutions that solve these problems.

This is different from the traditional approach to project management,
which focuses on tame and messy uncertainty. The traditional approach is based
on designing processes that identify a whole, disaggregate it into component
parts, provide information on the component parts and integrate the parts back
together while accounting for potential risks along the way. This approach
limits the Solution Delivery Capabilities of the Project Environment and the
range of potential participants involved in the Solution Delivery Process. It
constrains the courses of action which people can take to find solutions and
who will be involved in finding those solutions.

The traditional approach has value. Tame and messy issues are real and
affect the type of solutions which an environment can deliver. Approaches
oriented toward tame and messy uncertainty deliver successful outcomes
given a specific set of circumstances and under specific operating conditions.
However, approaches oriented toward wicked uncertainty have wider
applicability and create different Solution Delivery Capabilities within an
environment. Further, approaches oriented toward wicked uncertainty,
when integrated into traditional environments, change the Solution Delivery
Capabilities of that environment. Approaches oriented toward wicked
uncertainty have a better chance of delivering desired outcomes since
approaches oriented toward wickedness more accurately match the underlying
nature of the problem being addressed.

---

3   Ibid., pp. 176–7.

Communication is the key to accurately matching an environment's Solution Delivery Capabilities with the underlying nature of the problem. Since all uncertainty is ultimately wicked, that is, it stems from people making decisions, having potentially competing interests in the project and having different orientations, communication can help us to manage project performance. And with technology now allowing us to observe, analyze and study communication in a more empirical manner, we can be more exact when managing project performance using communication.

This has implications for people who work in Project Environments, people who manage projects and people who design Project Environments.

WHAT IT MEANS TO PEOPLE WHO WORK IN PROJECT ENVIRONMENTS

For people who work in Project Environments, this means that we can improve the effectiveness of the work we do by understanding the wicked nature of the environments we operate in. We need to recognize that a project is a social environment. We can tailor our communications to account for the environment using the elements of Communication Objects and can use an awareness of the Communication Design of the environment and its orientation toward uncertainty to make more informed decisions within the environment. We can also increase our value to other participants by aligning our efforts with the goals of other people in the environment or helping align other people's efforts with the goals of the Project Environment.

WHAT IT MEANS FOR PEOPLE WHO MANAGE PROJECT ENVIRONMENTS

For people who manage projects, we can improve the Solution Delivery Capabilities of our Project Environments by understanding how our environments behave with respect to Communication Design decisions and Communication Object Elements. We can observe the connection between specific design decisions and Project Environment behaviors, and the connection between specific Communication Object elements and Project Environment behaviors. We can use these observations to tailor our design and object decisions to encourage the types of behaviors we would like to see in our Project Environments. Similarly, we can observe and draw connections between the design and object elements and individual behaviors to help us tailor our management of specific individuals.

As project managers, we can turn this same analysis toward the larger institutional context in which our Project Environments operate. We can use an awareness of the Communication Design of the larger environment in which our project operates, and its orientation toward uncertainty, to improve the way we work with stakeholders and within the constraints of the larger environment in which our project operates. We can increase our value to stakeholders by aligning our efforts with their goals and can increase our effectiveness within the larger environment by accounting for the constraints and opportunities of the larger environment when building our Solution Delivery Processes.

For example, there are corporate research and development departments that come up with products without understanding the needs of their company's customers. The products may be great, but they stay on the shelves of the research and development department because nobody knows how to sell them or what they could be used for. In contrast, when researchers have a chance to interact with customers or with people who understand the customers, such as salespeople or customer support technicians, they have a better chance of coming up with products that can be sold to customers.

Here is another example. There are weapons engineers and strategists who argue for changing the caliber of standard-issue service rifles in the US military. The arguments may be sound; however, the movement has trouble moving toward implementation. The current caliber is produced around the country, in the home states and congressional districts of many members of Congress. The technical merits of changing caliber may compete with the interests of the constituents of the members of Congress. This is the type of non-convergent range of solution sets typical of wicked uncertainty. The weapons engineers and strategists can improve their chances of implementing a rifle with the improved characteristics they see from having a different caliber by including the Congress people and their constituents in the Solution Delivery Process.

WHAT IT MEANS FOR PEOPLE WHO DESIGN PROJECT ENVIRONMENTS

For people who design Project Environments, we can design our Project Environments for desired Solution Delivery Capabilities by understanding the interplay between Solution Delivery Capabilities and Communication Design decisions, Communication Object Element decisions and orientation toward uncertainty. We can increase our understanding of the ripple effects of any specific set of Solution Delivery Capabilities under consideration. We can analyze the potential constraints the desired Solution Delivery Capabilities place on other parts of the Project Environment. We can then use Communication Design decisions, Communication Object elements and changes in the orientation toward uncertainty to work through the constraints and facilitate achieving the desired Solution Delivery Capabilities.

For example, the leaders in the Heathrow Terminal 5 case study determined that the traditional approach to decision making constrained project participants from adequately reducing risk to an acceptable level. The traditional approach failed to provide sufficient mitigation against a potential failure such as that which was seen in the collapse of the Heathrow Express tunnel in 1994. The leaders implemented a change in the orientation toward uncertainty by changing the content of the Communication Object—the mission statement—which they changed to include the phrase "respecting last responsible moment." This had a ripple effect throughout the Project Environment and changed the environment's Solution Delivery Capabilities. The Solution Delivery Capabilities more accurately matched the underlying nature of the source of risk, namely, wicked uncertainty. Being more accurately matched, the Solution Delivery Capabilities of the Project Environment produced the desired outcome. As such, the development project was a success.

The F/A-18 E/F program is another good example where the Communication Environment accurately matched the desired outcomes of the project. The leaders of the program understood that they needed to deliver a product that seamlessly integrated numerous components and had many different stakeholders. They determined that a traditional approach to program management would constrain their ability to deliver the seamlessly integrated product and would also constrain their ability to work with the numerous different stakeholders. They implemented a change in the Communication Design of the environment, creating an environment of seamless communication using a well-defined set of Communication Objects to keep all stakeholders on the same page. This had a ripple effect throughout the Project Environment and changed the environment's Solution Delivery Capabilities. The Solution Delivery Capabilities more accurately matched the desired outcome, a seamlessly integrated product. Being more accurately matched, the program delivered the desired outcome and the program was a success.

IMPACT ON SOLUTION DELIVERY CAPABILITIES

The design of the Communication Environment directly impacts Solution Delivery Capabilities. Accuracy matters when designing the Communication Environment. If the desired outcome is innovation, gear your environment to the necessary characteristics to innovate; if the desired outcome is market share, gear your environment to that; if the desired outcome is dominance over an adversary, gear your environment to that. It is people operating in the social construct of a Project Environment who are at the root of a Project Environment's Solution Delivery Capabilities. Therefore, we need to use a Performance Management Toolset that is oriented toward people and the social environment of projects. Communication, as described in this book, is this tool for performance management. We can use it to design, plan, control, manage and lead our Project Environments to deliver specific Solution Delivery Capabilities and desired outcomes.

Epilogue

The book started out with a discussion on the role people play in delivering project outcomes. We are going to end with a discussion on the role people play in today's competitive environment. This discussion is germane to the economic marketplace as well as to the competitive threat environment countries now operate in.

Organizations operate in an environment with numerous competitors, who utilize a myriad of tactics and technologies. There are few predictable bounds to the ways in which organizations will compete. Using a national security context, the threat environment is hybrid, with numerous proxies in an unconventional domain with a near-infinite range of motion by adversaries. An organization's range of motion is limited by its Communication Structure. An environment whose Solution Delivery Capabilities are bound by a dependence on prediction and development of solutions using processes geared toward tame and messy problems will produce different outcomes from an environment that is oriented toward wickedness. The threat environment is wicked. The ability to react and provide capability overmatch is dependent on people, not processes; therefore, we need to structure our Communication Environments appropriately. We cannot rely on prediction or measure for prediction, but rather, as in the Heathrow Terminal 5 example, should create relationships that allow us to react at the last responsible moment. Project Environments oriented toward wicked uncertainty more accurately reflect the nature of the underlying problem we are trying to solve. Organizations that seek to solve problems in these environments and that are oriented toward wicked uncertainty will produce different outcomes from those that are oriented toward tame and messy uncertainty. We cannot rely on patterns or prediction. We need to rely on people and use communication as a Performance Management Tool to design environments that have the Solution Delivery Capabilities we require to solve the most pressing problems of our age.

People have never been more empowered than they are today. One person, with an Internet connection, can change the world. A person in the farthest reaches of the world can communicate with and learn from someone across the globe—and, because of the magic of translation software, these people don't even need to speak the same language. One can learn almost anything on YouTube and can connect with anyone with the same interests. Groups of people can organize uprisings against traditional totalitarian governments. And a group of hacktivists can take down critical infrastructure from their basements, sitting thousands of miles apart from each other.

The empowerment doesn't end with the Internet. There has never been greater access to off-the-shelf technology that does incredible things, and most of them with easy-to-use interfaces. Further, one doesn't even need to be a trained specialist to use it; it is easy for laypeople to conceive of new ways to put component technologies together and it is easy for these people to put them together with great effect. This was evident in the battlespace with Improvised Explosive Devices (IEDs) and the cat-and-mouse game between the bomb makers and the national army. The bomb makers figured out how to make IEDs using common materials and inflict damage on the army. Soldiers figured out how to rig together a simple sweeper made out of a pole and toaster oven[4] to pre-detonate the IEDs. The bomb makers upped the ante. So did the soldiers.

The key element behind both of these trends is that there are empowered individuals. No longer does it take a large industrial base to create weapons or inflict damage. No longer does it take attendance at a prestigious university to gain the know-how or even access the latest research on a topic. No longer does it take employment at a large corporation to conduct research and

---

4   Adam Higginbotham, "U.S. Military Learns to Fight Deadliest Weapons," *Wired Magazine*, 28 July 2010, http://www.wired.com/magazine/2010/07/ff_roadside_bombs/all.

development on a new product. No longer does it take specialized knowledge to obtain and combine existing capabilities to develop incredible new ways of challenging the status quo. Everything is now within reach of the individual.

Wickedness has promulgated and is the new status quo. This means that in order for organizations to survive in today's environment, we need to adopt Solution Delivery Processes that are oriented toward wickedness. We need to unlock the potential of the individual and unbound and utilize that potential in the service of the organization's goals. There is nothing stopping every other actor in the competitive environment from doing so. We can use communication as a Performance Management Tool to design, plan and deliver Project Environments that are oriented toward wickedness and that give our organizations the highest likelihood of achieving their goals in the current competitive global environment.

Appendix
Case Study: An IT Department Supporting a Large Project

Here is an example of what Communication Objects and Object elements look like in a live project. It highlights the value of analyzing Communication Object elements as an indicator of people's behavior and how that analysis can facilitate management decisions to increase the probability of an organization or, in this case, department meeting its desired goals. It also demonstrates the importance of interpersonal relationships as well as the connection between decisions about the Communication Environment and the types of solutions an organization is capable of delivering, impacting the organization's prospects over the long term. The example is pulled from a real-life situation, but has been modified for reasons of confidentiality.

The IT department is part of a large, integrated project team. They are responsible for the maintenance and operations of the servers on the project. As part of their communication process, they utilize an integrated ticketing and issue management system. The integrated system sends out e-mails to the project manager whenever there is an update to the project manager's project servers.

Since the IT department does a very good job in keeping the servers going, the vast majority of the e-mails sent to the project manager concern do not require any input from the project manager. For example, here is a mock-up of the project manager's inbox showing e-mails from the IT department over a three-month period. The truncated subject line reflects the project manager's configuration of their inbox.

From	Subject	Received
IT Department	[Maintenance Notice] (Completed) – Scheduled D	Thu 3/8/2011 8:10 pm
IT Department	[Maintenance Notice] (Starting) – Scheduled Dow	Thu 3/8/2011 5:34 pm
IT Department	[Maintenance Notice] Scheduled Downtime Co	Thu 3/8/2011 2:19 pm
IT Department	[Impact Notice] Completed Management Mainten	Sat 2/12/2011 4:45 am
IT Department	[Impact Notice] Starting Management Maintenan	Sat 2/12/2011 2:17 am
IT Department	[Impact Notice] Scheduled Management Mainten	Fri 2/11/2011 10:27 am
IT Department	[Impact Notice] Completed/Failed/Rescheduled	Mon 1/24/2011 10:52 pm
IT Department	[Impact Notice] Starting Emergency Maintenance	Mon 1/24/2011 8:28 pm
IT Department	RESOLUTION NOTICE OF SCHEDULED MAINTENAN	Tue 1/11/2011 2:53 pm
IT Department	IMPACT NOTICE OF SCHEDULED MAINTENANCE	Tue 1/11/2011 12:06 pm

Here are the details of a few of the usual e-mails.

SUBJECT: [Impact Notice] Completed Management Maintenance

SENT: Sat 2/12/2011 4:45 am

To Project Manager,

This is the final notice about the previously communicated scheduled maintenance.

Results:

The communicated changes have been completed.

If you have any questions regarding this notice, please contact support directly by logging into the ticketing system or replying to this e-mail.

Thank you,
The IT Department

SUBJECT: [Impact Notice] Starting Management Maintenance

SENT: Sat 2/12/2011 2:17 am

To Project Manager,

This is a proactive notice to let you know we will be starting the previously communicated scheduled maintenance within the next 30 minutes. Another notice will be sent once the work has been completed.

If you have any questions regarding this notice, please contact support directly by logging into the ticketing system or replying to this e-mail.

Thank you,
The IT Department

As we can see, the IT department broadcasts about once or twice a month. It generally sends out three e-mails: one to announce an upcoming action; one to announce the beginning of the action; and one to announce the end of the action. The e-mails do not require any intervention by the project manager; the issues are announced and resolved by the IT department on their own. Over time, the project manager has come to simply delete e-mails from the IT department.

On a Monday, the project manager was traveling out of the office for project-related business. She checked her inbox from her phone and noticed that there was an e-mail from the IT department.

From	Subject	Received
IT Department	[Impact Notice] Server Compromised – Incident 5691-12	Mon 2/6/2012 2:54 pm

The project manager would usually delete the e-mail, but the subject line looked different from the usual e-mails. The IT department had been known to change subject lines over time for no known reason to the project manager, but the project manager decided not to delete the e-mail and to look at it later; she had a meeting to attend at the moment.

Later in the evening, at around 6:00 pm, she read the e-mail. This is what it said.

SUBJECT: [Impact Notice] Server Compromised – Incident 5691-12
SENT: Mon 2/6/2012 2:54 pm
To Project Manager, Recently you requested personal assistance from online support. Below is a summary of your request and our response. We are continuing to work on your issue. If you have more information, update your question here.

Discussion Thread	
Response (Richard Brooks)	02/06/2012 02:54 PM

Hello,

Over the weekend we observed the project servers communicating with an outside malicious server. After investigating we have determined the servers are severely infected.

The ultimate point of entry appears to be through exploitation of a vulnerability in the web server software system this past August (at the time, a 0 day vulnerability) that allowed an attacker to bypass authentication into the administrator and create a malicious shell under the main directory. This shell has been utilized since to create and execute many malicious processes.

Because of the scope of the infection, the servers will need to be replaced. The hardware procurement group is being contacted so that we may begin the process of issuing replacements. We were able to "clean" the servers enough to allow them to remain active on the network temporarily while all project content is migrated to the replacements or until further malicious activity is observed.

You can refer to the comments below for further details into our investigation of the servers. The hardware procurement group should be in contact with you shortly regarding the replacement process.

Thank you.

Client (Entered by Richard Brooks)	02/06/2012 02:44 PM

Because the degree of severity of the virus, this server will need to get replaced.

I've removed as much of the virus as I could identify and find so that the server can stay online with all the content is moved to a replacement server.

Client (Entered by Richard Brooks)	02/06/2012 02:42 PM

- Server found to be infected with a contagious virus.

If you have any questions regarding this notice, please contact support directly by logging into the ticketing system or replying to this e-mail.

Thank you,
The IT Department

The project manager came away with the impression that the IT department was doing their usual excellent job of keeping things going, that there were no risks to her project and that no input was needed from her. This impression was based on her past experiences with communication from the IT department as well as from the following information gleaned from the content of the e-mail:

- The issue was detected over the weekend and she was not notified; therefore, it must be low risk and manageable by the IT department.

- The issue was detected over the weekend and the IT department was only getting to it now, on Monday afternoon; therefore, it must be low risk and not very pressing.

- The e-mail thread stated that the IT department had already set a process in motion to get the replacement servers; therefore, no action was needed on her part.

- The e-mail was said to be in response to a request made by the project team to online support, yet the original entry was made by Richard Brooks, who is in the IT department and is not part of her task delivery team. Therefore, the IT department was "faking" the interaction with the client in order to log the issue in the issue management system, but no interaction was really necessary.

To confirm this last point, the project manager called the lead on her task delivery team to ask if he or anyone from the team had contacted the IT department with an issue over the weekend or today. He checked around and replied that nobody had. This confirmed her impression that this was an internal interaction within the IT department.

To be on the safe side, the project manager engaged in a conversation with the IT department. In the conversation she checked on the safety of the project data stored in the servers, got further confirmation of her impression that no action was needed on her part and thanked the IT department for always being on top of issues.

This is what the response thread looked like.

SUBJECT: [Impact Notice] Server Compromised – Incident 5691-12
SENT: Mon 2/6/2012 6:59 pm
To Project Manager,   Recently you requested personal assistance from online support. Below is a summary of your request and our response.   We are continuing to work on your issue. If you have more information, update your question here.

Discussion Thread	
Client (Project Manager)	02/06/2012 06:59 PM
Thank you for your fantastic support. Do we need to do anything at our end?	
Response (Laura Sanchez)	02/06/2012 06:53 PM
We can't really know what was accessed, if anything. But this type of virus is used to turn the servers into nodes for malicious activity to contact and infect other servers on the Internet. It isn't usually used to get data. The virus has been contained. The servers could be targeted and infected again and it would begin again all other again. The malicious traffic from the servers has stopped and that is why we are keeping the servers online until everything can be migrated to the new servers. We'll keep following up and updating you as the new servers are procured from inventory, set-up and brought online.	
Client (Project Manager)	02/06/2012 06:37 PM
Thanks for your e-mail. Has any of the project data stored in the servers or the software code being utilized, been compromised, stolen or threatened? Have the current servers been secured to stop another infection? If you have any questions regarding this notice, please contact support directly by logging into the ticketing system or replying to this e-mail. Thank you, The IT Department	

The project manager didn't hear anything back from the IT department before she had to leave at 7:30 pm for a dinner meeting. She figured that no news was good news and left feeling confirmed in her understanding that the IT department had everything under control. She scanned an e-mail that came in from the IT department at around 8:30 pm. The IT department had moved quickly to get new servers procured from inventory and was in the process of getting them set up. It mentioned some activity that her team would need to coordinate later. Everything continued to appear to be under control without risk to the project.

When the project manager returned to the hotel around 10:30 pm, she checked her e-mail and was shocked by what she read.

SUBJECT: [Impact Notice] Server Compromised – Incident 5691-12
SENT: Mon 2/6/2012 10:04 pm
To Project Manager, Recently you requested personal assistance from online support. Below is a summary of your request and our response. We are continuing to work on your issue. If you have more information, update your question here.

Discussion Thread	
Response (Alfonso Cevasco)	02/06/2012 10:04 PM
Per our previous communications, the infected servers will be left online until you can migrate everything to the new servers. It is important for you to know that if the malicious activity begins again on the old servers, the project servers will be taken offline. Thomas Morozov will reach out to you tomorrow to follow-up.	
Response (Thomas Morozov)	02/06/2012 08:21 PM
My name is Thomas Morozov. I am in charge of managing the procurement, set-up, build and installation of your new servers. The servers have been procured and have gone to set-up and build. At this point, there is not anything for you to do. Once the servers are brought online, a set-up share will be established between the new servers and the old servers. We will then hand it over to you and your team will need to arrange for a transfer of files between the new servers and the old servers. We can help by answering any questions about the process or guidelines for the new servers. Feel free to contact me with any questions. When we have an update on the status of the new servers, we will send you that information. If you have any questions regarding this notice, please contact support directly by logging into the ticketing system or replying to this e-mail. Thank you, The IT Department	

The latest e-mail said that the project servers could be taken offline at any point. This now became a major risk to the project. Needless to say, the project manager was not happy to read that; her risk management plan relied on the IT department being accountable for server-related risks. She listed potential impacts on her end, determined what information would be helpful for her to obtain and called the IT department to get further information. Most importantly, she wanted to understand the probability that the servers would be taken offline and what mitigation efforts could be put in place.

When she called, she got the night crew. After a frustrating 15-minute conversation, it was clear that she and the night crew were speaking different languages. They were not able to give her a probability that the servers could be taken offline and they didn't understand why it would be important to her anyway. They were focused on conveying the messages that they had no way of knowing if and when malicious activity could start again, that the servers could be taken offline at any point and that she should call Thomas Morozov tomorrow to follow-up on the migration plan. They had no way of contacting him this evening. She did not make any headway on the probability or mitigation efforts. All she was able to do was to get them to agree to notify her, via a phone call, before the servers would be taken offline, no matter what time of day or night.

She hung-up with the night crew and begrudgingly called her team leader. It was now 11:15 pm. She apologized for calling him so late and let him know that the servers could be taken offline at any point in time and that there was no mitigation plan. She asked him to check on the status of the offsite server back-ups which she had procured independently of the IT department. The team leader confirmed that the back-ups were running smoothly, were up to date and were available for a restore onto new machines should the project servers go down. This was a relief to her and a testament to her planning. In the worst-case scenario, if the servers were taken offline, her team and customers would lose some time, but they would not lose data. She told him that no further action was needed right now and asked him to be ready to send out a message to the project team if she got the call that the servers were being taken offline, which he agreed to do. She planned the calls she would need to make to the stakeholders and project customers if the servers were taken offline. She then prepared to cancel all her scheduled appointments for the next day. She did not sleep much that night.

As the hours passed, the servers remained online.

Early in the morning, she fired-off an e-mail to the most senior person she knew at the IT department. She asked for a call as early as possible. He called her right away. Together, on the phone, they reviewed the situation. He was able to tell her that the probability of the servers being taken offline was very, very low. The original engineer who had cleaned the servers had done an excellent job. He got Thomas Morozov on the line to get a sense of the schedule for having the new servers up and ready. Together they mapped out a target timeline for the migration and the steps that would need to be taken. By the end of the call, it became clear that there was no urgency in terms of doing the migration—a risk remained, but it was being managed.

She got off the call and called the team leader to update him on the situation. Together they put together a plan for the migration with clear next steps. She thanked him for being available last night. She then went to her appointments that day as scheduled. To complete the story, the servers remained online without a problem for another five weeks until the migration was completed.

Long-Term Impact

The incident had a long-term impact on the project manager and her team. Most directly, it reduced her trust in the IT department; one sleepless night can do that. Consequently, she began looking at outside providers who she could directly communicate with to meet the needs which the IT department provided.

The incident also directly affected the Solution Delivery Capabilities of the project manager's team and reinforced her perception of the IT department as a service bureau. She was not alone in this perception—all the project managers shared this perception and it affected the Solution Delivery Capabilities of project teams throughout the organization.

The IT department was designed and set up like a utility to provide a needed service for projects. It focused on providing hardware, networking and connectivity. It was not, and could not be, an integrated part of a project team. As a result, project managers never considered hardware, connectivity or networking as areas that could contribute to an innovative solution; they were simply necessary components of a project, like having lights and electricity. They would no more call IT and ask for their input on a potential project than they would call up the electricity company. The areas that the IT department focused on were not value-added areas for innovative solutions.

Project managers in the organization focused on software and process improvements to deliver solutions. They never would think of providing an integrated hardware and software solution that leveraged embedded circuits or hardware optimized for a specific purpose; hardware, connectivity and networking were simply a layer that solutions had to sit on. Because of this, project managers began looking more at cloud-based solutions in order to meet their project needs. After all, if someone outside the organization could provide the same utility at a lower price and with better responsiveness, it would benefit the organization's bottom line. The IT department's focus on being an efficient service bureau paved the road for their own irrelevance.

Further, by looking at software-only solutions, the organization missed out solutions that potentially offered higher margins and a more competitive position in the market. Integrated hardware and software solutions can be faster and more efficient than a software-only solution, making them more attractive for specific uses by customers. Because they contain hardware, they can leverage economies of scale from industrial production. Integrated solutions offer a more defensible market position since they can provide a greater barrier to entry against competition compared to software only products, which are more highly portable. By operating the IT department as an efficient service bureau, the organization missed out on these benefits.

Analysis Using Communication as a Performance Management Tool

The impact of the organization's Communication Environment on its Solution Delivery Capabilities can be analyzed using the Communication Object Elements. The goal of the current Communication Environment was to broadcast out information about known issues which could affect a client's projects. Since the IT department uses an automated ticket and issue management system which generates e-mails, we can study the e-mails generated. A good analytic tool to measure the effectiveness of the goal would be to compare the number of known issues against the number of e-mails sent about the issue. An example of fictional data for this measurement is displayed in Figure A.1.

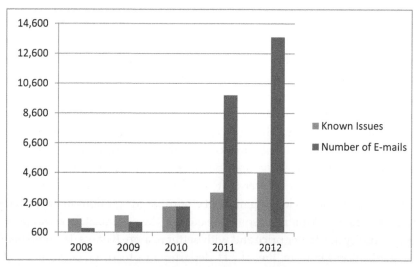

Figure A.1   A Comparison of Known Issues with Numbers of E-mails

This first thing we learn from the data in Figure A.1 is the growth in the number of known issues. This is a result of the growth of the organization and increased use of the IT department's services as the organization grew. Known issues grew from 1,500 in 2008 to nearly 4,600 in 2012.

We also see the evolution of the communication system over this period of time. In 2008, there were 800 e-mails sent out for the 1,500 known issues. E-mails were sent 57 percent of the time. Information was falling through the cracks and people were being caught off-guard. Even if most of the issues didn't affect project managers, all it would take would be one big mishap that could have been prevented with advance warning to kick off a corporate-wide initiative to change the system. In 2009, roughly 1,300 e-mails were sent out covering 75 percent of the 1,725 issues during the year. In 2010, every single known issue was covered in an e-mail—there were 2,329 issues and 2,329 e-mails. These were advance notifications before the issue actually occurred.

However, the leaders determined that this was not sufficient information. They implemented a program to send out advance notification, notification of when the issue was starting and notification of when the issue was resolved. This resulted in three e-mails being sent for each known issue. Because the system of matching e-mails to issues had been perfected in 2010, it was relatively easy for the IT department to scale from 1:1 to 3:1. As we can see in Figure A.1, in 2011 and 2012 there were three e-mails for every one known issue. This resulted in 9,781 e-mails in 2011 for the 3,260 known issues and nearly 13,700 issues in 2012 for the 4,564 known issues.

The program of having three e-mails for every known issue did a good job in terms of broadcasting information. Never again could anyone say that they were not sufficiently apprised of known issues and their potential impact on their project servers. However, while this was a success for the goal of broadcasting information, it also created a massive influx of communication to project managers, most of it irrelevant. It thus resulted in a system where as the organization grew and the need for the IT department's services grew, the amount of communication from the department increased threefold. So, despite the growing importance of the IT department as a service provider, communications from the IT department were being increasingly ignored.

We can see this by looking at the open rates for e-mails from the IT department over time. An example of fictional data for this estimated trend is shown in Figure A.2.

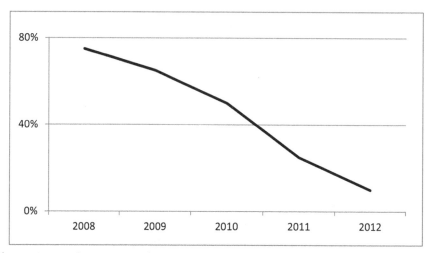

Figure A.2   Open Rates for E-mails over Time

This data shows that as the number of e-mails from the IT department increased, fewer and fewer of them were being opened. This is a testament to the consistent performance of the IT department as a service bureau—they were taking care of business, keeping everything running and under control without catching anyone's attention, and had successfully made the IT department into a seamless utility for the organization.

Being successful in this goal, however, had an impact. The Communication Environment was meeting its goal of notifying project managers, but was failing in other ways. Consider the need to have the IT department be a trusted part of a project team, a team player with whom other team members communicated, rather than being a service provider. Were the goal to have IT be an integrated part of a project team, we could still use the same Communication Object of the e-mails from the automated ticket and issue tracking system, but we would apply a different analytic tool. We would look at the reply rate of each e-mail. Each e-mail solicits interaction from the recipient. It allows a recipient to engage in a conversation with the IT department by logging into the ticket system or by replying directly to the e-mail just as one would with any e-mail sent from a person.

We can see this by looking at the reply rates for e-mails from the IT department over time. An example of fictional data for this estimated trend is shown in Figure A.3. The data starts in 2010, which is when the current automated system was implemented.

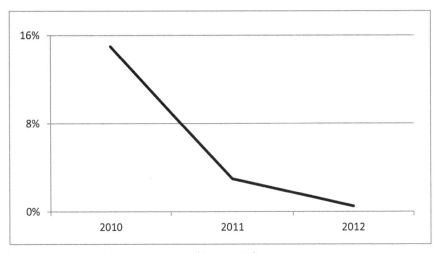

Figure A.3   Reply Rates to E-mails over Time

Here we see the consequences of the Communication Environment. The significant increase in the number of e-mails and the fall in open rates translates directly into a near-zero level of interaction between project team members and the IT department. A project team member would only reply to the IT department if something were wrong. As such, any interaction with the IT department was biased toward negative risk from the outset. It didn't take long for an interaction with the IT department to reinforce the image that the IT department was filled with tech geeks who provided little value to projects and who could not contribute to innovative solutions.

The IT department was successfully placed in a silo and cut off from being an integrated member of project teams. This directly impacts the organization's Solution Delivery Capabilities. This could be predicted using an analysis of the e-mails as Communication Objects and applying the analytic tool that best matches the desired goals of the Project Environment. In this way, communication can be used as a performance management tool. The next step to improving the performance of the Project Environment is to vary Communication Object Elements, such as the number of e-mails per known issue, the frequency of communication, the target recipient or the contents of the e-mail, and measure the changes against the analytic tool, for example, in the case study above, seeing how a change in the frequency of e-mails sent to the project manager changes the response rates to those e-mails.

Index

A COM, 74–7, 79–80, 90, 96; *see also* Actual Communication

Abba, Wayne, 17

Actual Communication, 69, 72, 74, 78, 90, 96; *see also* A COM

artifacts, 4, 23, 34, 39–40

audience, 40–41, 44–5, 48, 50–51, 53, 61, 66–7, 125

battlespace, 137; *see also* Epilogue

Bliss, Gary, 16

boundary, 41, 51–4, 60, 62, 66–7, 73, 114, 125, 127

boundary object, 41, 53, 60, 66–7, 114, 125, 127

Boyd, John C., 3, 122–3; *see also* OODA

choice, 4, 7, 19, 23, 41, 46, 48, 66–7, 92, 99–100, 104, 125, 129, 131

COM V, 74–81, 90, 96; *see also* Communication Variance

Communication Design, 5, 14, 16–18, 21–3, 25, 27, 29, 34, 36–7, 39, 59–60, 67, 69, 81–2, 86–8, 93, 95, 125–6, 133–5

Communication Environment, 4–5, 13–14, 19, 21–2, 25–6, 32, 36–7, 39–41, 52, 55–6, 60, 62, 65–7, 74, 76, 81–2, 86, 91–2, 95, 103–4, 117, 124–5, 135–6, 139, 148, 151

Communication Object Elements, 9, 41, 55, 66, 81, 83, 86, 99–102, 133, 135, 151; *see also* Elements of Communication Objects

Communication Objects, 9, 39–41, 43, 46, 48, 50, 52–5, 57–9, 61, 66–7, 86, 98–100, 103, 124–5, 127, 133, 135, 139, 151

Communication Strategy, 21, 32–3, 44, 59, 66, 70–72, 80–81, 87–9, 91, 125

Communication Structure, 26, 132, 136

Communication Variance, 74, 96; *see also* COM V

communicationmeasurement.org, 9

competitive, 7–9, 104, 114–15, 123, 136, 138, 148

competitors, 136

complexity, 16, 105, 109, 131–2

constraints, 4, 6, 19, 22, 26–7, 95, 126, 130, 134–5

Conway, Melvin, 13–14, 16–17, 19, 21, 25, 37, 132

Cost Performance Index, 58; *see also* CPI

Cost Variance, 58; *see also* CV

CPI, 58; *see also* Cost Performance Index

Csikszentmihalyi, Mihaly, 48

culture, 52

CV, 58; *see also* Cost Variance

decision making, 3, 24, 53, 67, 104,
    110, 120, 123, 135
Design Elements, 21, 37, 58, 66, 81, 93,
    101–3, 124–5, 128
domain, 32, 92, 102, 136
Dyer, Joseph W., 16–17

Earned Value Management, 16, 58; *see
    also* EVM
economics, 92
Elements of Communication Design,
    21, 36, 60, 86, 125
Elements of Communication Objects,
    41, 66–7, 86, 124, 133; *see
    also* Communication Object
    Elements
Epilogue, 9, 136
EVM, 16–17, 61–2, 69–70, 74, 76, 83–4,
    89, 119, 125, 131
expectations, 115, 119

F/A - 18 E/F, 16–18, 22, 61, 111, 114,
    135
feedback, 22, 33, 60, 119, 127
flexibility, 14, 112–13, 115–17, 119,
    122–5, 127
Fold.it, 65, 111
forecast, 79–80, 83–4, 91, 120

Gates, Bill, 121–2
Godin, Seth, 42–3, 45, 94
Google, 93, 97

Hancock, David, 54, 62–3, 108, 110–11
Heathrow Terminal 5, 62, 109–10,
    120, 135–6
Hertogh, Marcel, 131
Higginbotham, Adam, 137

Holt, Robin, 54, 62–3, 108, 110–11
How to Use this Book, 8
human behavior, 7, 129–31

ICS, 32–6; *see also* Integrated
    Communication Strategy
innovative, 57, 147, 151
institutional context, 65, 134
Integrated Communication Strategy,
    21, 32, 71, 88–9, 91; *see also* ICS

Lackey, James, 17
Lincoln, President Abraham, 53

marketing, 47
marketspace, 8
Mars Orbiter, 25, 52, 109
MCA, 87, 95; *see also* Measurable
    Communication Action
McChrystal, Stanley, 53
Measurable Communication Action,
    87; *see also* MCA
Messy, 54, 62, 108–14, 118–20, 123–4,
    129–30, 132, 136–7
methods of communication, 21, 26,
    70, 82, 95–7, 101
Microsoft, 46, 59, 65, 121–2
mission statement, 61–4, 135

Object Elements, 9, 41, 55, 58–9, 66,
    81–3, 86, 92, 97, 99–103, 128,
    133, 135, 139, 151
observable behaviors, 57–8, 67, 86, 92,
    94, 98–101, 103, 112
observable elements, 59, 62, 98
Observable Manifestations, 112, 124–5
OODA, 3, 122; *see also* Boyd, John C.
Orientation Toward Uncertainty,
    107–10, 112–14, 120, 123–5, 128,
    130, 133–5

oversight, 26, 113–14, 116–17,
     127–8

P COM, 74–7, 90, 96; *see also* Planned
     Communication
perceptions, 3, 63, 109
Performance Management Tool, 1,
     7–9, 36, 67, 69, 76, 81, 83, 85–7,
     91, 95–6, 101–4, 124,
     137–8, 148, 151
Performance Measurement Baseline,
     23, 70, 72, 119; *see also* PMB
personality, 81
Planned Communication, 74, 78, 81–2,
     87–90, 96; *see also* P COM
PMB, 23, 70, 72, 84, 119; *see also*
     Performance Measurement
     Baseline
prediction, 7–8, 114–17, 119–20, 125,
     136–7
probability, 35, 47, 63–4, 79, 108–9,
     145–6
Project Environment Participants, 107,
     109, 111
project performance, 5–7, 14, 58, 61,
     63, 66, 69, 73, 76, 79, 81, 83–5,
     90–91, 97, 102–4, 113,
     119–20, 125, 133
Project Performance Management, 6,
     69, 102
psychology, 48, 56

regulations, 61
resilience, 124–5
Revealed Preferences, 92
risk management, 54, 62–3, 110–11,
     130, 145
risk register, 54, 63–4
risk workshop, 62–3, 120
root cause, 19, 76–7, 83–4, 91, 102

schedule performance, 6, 58–9, 75–6,
     81–2, 88–90
Schedule Performance Index, 58; *see
     also* SPI
Schedule Variance, 57; *see also* SV
Schwarzkopf, Norman, 1, 3
scope, 39, 54, 114–15, 127, 130, 142
Second and Third Order, 81
social, 1, 7, 36, 64, 81–2, 91, 102, 104,
     131, 133, 136
social issues, 81
sociology, 56
Solution Delivery Capabilities, 9, 28,
     36–7, 39, 54, 56, 60–61, 65, 67,
     76, 83, 86, 92–3, 95, 103, 108,
     110, 112–13, 116, 118, 121, 124,
     126–8, 130, 132–7, 147
Solution Delivery Process, 28–9, 33,
     113–14, 120, 132
span of control, 6, 87
SPI, 58–9, 69, 125, 127; *see also*
     Schedule Performance Index
Spotlight, 9, 15, 24, 29, 47, 50, 53, 65,
     81, 93, 101, 122, 126
stakeholder, 64, 81, 130–31
Star, Susan Leigh, 17, 53, 92
Stewart, Jon, 53
Structure, 13, 19, 22–3, 25–6, 32–3, 115,
     122, 127, 132, 136
Structure of the Communication
     Environment, 25
SV, 57–9; *see also* Schedule Variance
system design, 14

Tame, 54, 62, 108–14, 118–20, 123–4,
     129–30, 132, 136–7
technical performance, 16, 36, 92
trust, 17, 56–7, 111, 117, 147

US Army, 126, 137

US Congress, 16, 134
US Department of Defense, 18, 26
US Government, 13–14, 16–17, 25, 61,
        108, 111, 114
US Military, 3, 17, 53, 117, 134, 137
US Navy, 16
US Postal Service, 121
uniqueness, 94–5

Vanhoucke, Mario, 24
visibility, 28, 111, 120–23, 125

WBS, 23; *see also* Work Breakdown
        Structure

Weiler, Edward, 18
Westerveld, Eddy, 131
What it Means for Us, 9, 19, 34, 55, 66,
        83, 102, 124, 132
Wicked, 9, 54, 62, 108–13, 118, 121,
        123–4, 127, 129–34, 136–7
Work Breakdown Structure, 23; *see
        also* WBS
workflow, 21, 31–2, 66, 125

X–Prize, 65, 111

Zarrella, Dan, 42–3, 45, 94

.

For Product Safety Concerns and Information please contact our
EU representative GPSR@taylorandfrancis.com Taylor & Francis
Verlag GmbH, Kaufingerstraße 24, 80331 München, Germany